# Report of the Select Committee of the House of Representatives, Appointed Under the Resolution of January 6, 1873

A. Yes. The stock was really not worth to the contractor who took it at par by any means, because it could be always bought in the market as low generally as from thirty to forty dollars.

Q. Then, if the $100 in stock was only worth about thirty or forty dollars to the contractor to whom it was paid, in proportioning what he rendered to the company between what was given as an equivalent for its stock and what was given as an equivalent for its Government bonds, and what was given as an equivalent for its own first-mortgage bonds, he did not render to the company $100 in value for every $100 in stock, did he?

A. No, sir.

Q. Was there any actual going through the ceremonial of paying in cash on those subscriptions to the treasurer of the Union Pacific Railroad Company?

A. Yes, there was always a check given.

Q. But the money never got into the treasury of the Union Pacific Railroad Company, I suppose?

A. The Union Pacific Railroad Company gave the trustees a check for the amount due, and the trustees turned over that check in payment to the Union Pacific Railroad Company for stock.

Q. There never was any interval between the payment of this check for stock and handing of it over again in payment of the contract?

A. Probably not.

Q. When you made, in behalf of the Union Pacific Railroad Company, the contract with Mr. Oakes Ames as contractor, you expected that the transaction which you have now described would be the substance of the transaction that would take place, did you not?

A. Substantially.

This contract extended over one hundred and thirty-eight miles of road completed and accepted. No work was done under it until after its assignment. That portion already completed had cost not to exceed $27,500 per mile, and by embracing this one hundred and thirty-eight miles in it, these trustees derived a "profit," if such a term is admissible in such a connection, which enabled them to make a dividend among the stockholders in less than sixty days after the assignment, namely, on the 12th of December, 1867, as follows: Sixty per cent. in first-mortgage bonds of the Union Pacific Railroad Company, $2,244,000; sixty per cent. in stock of the Union Pacific Railroad Company, $2,244,000.

This was mainly, if not entirely, derived from the excess of the contract price over what the one hundred and thirty-eight miles had cost.

The trustees proceeded to construct the road under this contract, and from a balance-sheet taken from the books it appears that the cost to the

| | |
|---|---|
| Railroad company was | $57, 140, 102 74 |
| And the cost to the contractors was | 27, 285, 141 99 |
| Profit | 29, 854, 141 99 |

The nature of this profit, as in case of that on the Hoxie contract, will appear hereafter. The next step in construction was under what is known as the

DAVIS CONTRACT.

This was a contract made with J. W. Davis, a man of but little, if any, pecuniary ability, (and not expected to perform the contract,) for the construction of that part of the road beginning at the western terminus of the "Ames contract," and extending to the western terminus of the road, a distance of one hundred and twenty-five and twenty-three hundredths miles. It was upon the same terms as the Ames contract, and was assigned to the same board of trustees. Under it the residue of the road was constructed, and, from a balance-sheet taken from the books of the railroad company, it appears that it

AN ACT to amend an act entitled "An act to aid in the construction of a railroad and telegraph line from the Missouri River to the Pacific Ocean, and to secure to the Government the use of the same for postal, military, and other purposes," and to secure the interests of the United States and of the people in the Union Pacific Railroad.

*Be it enacted by the Senate and House of Representatives of the United States of America n Congress assembled,* That the Attorney-General shall cause a suit in equity to be instituted in the name of the United States against the Union Pacific Railroad Company, and against all persons who may in their own names or through any agents have subscribed for or received capital stock in said road, which stock has not been paid for in full in money, or who may have received as dividends or otherwise portions of the capital stock of said road or the proceeds or avails thereof, or other property of said road, unlawfully and contrary to equity, or who may have received as profits or proceeds of contracts for construction or equipment of said road or other contracts therewith, moneys or other property which ought in equity to belong to said railroad corporation, or who may, under pretense of having complied with the acts to which this is an addition, have wrongfully and unlawfully received from the United States bonds, moneys, or lands, which ought in equity to be accounted for and paid to said railroad company or to the United States, and to compel payment for said stock, and the collection and payment of such moneys and the restoration of such property or its value either to said railroad corporation or to the United States, whichever shall in equity be held entitled thereto.

SEC. 2. That said suit may be brought in the circuit court in any circuit, and all said parties may be made defendants in one suit. Decrees may be entered and enforced against any one or more parties defendant without awaiting the final determination of the cause against other parties. The court where said cause is pending may make such orders and decrees and issue such process as it shall deem necessary to bring in new parties or the representatives of parties deceased, or to carry into effect the purposes of this act. On filing the bill, writs of capias and attachment may be issued by said court against any parties defendant, which writs shall run into any district, and shall be served as other like process by the marshal of such district, on which property, real and personal, may be attached to abide the event of the suit as like property may by law be attached on writs issuing from the circuit court in such district.

SEC. 3. That the books, records, correspondence, and all other documents of the Union Pacific Railroad Company shall at all times be open to inspection by the Secretary of the Treasury, or such persons as he may delegate for that purpose.

SEC. 4. That the laws of the United States providing for proceedings in bankruptcy shall not be held to apply to said corporation.

SEC. 5. That no dividend shall hereafter be made by said company but from the actual net earnings thereof, and no new stock shall be issued, or mortgages or pledges made on the property or future earnings of the company without leave of Congress, except for the purpose of funding and securing debts now existing, or the renewals thereof.

SEC. 6. That no director or officer of said road shall hereafter be interested, directly or indirectly, in any contract therewith, except for his lawful compensation as such officer.

SEC. 7. That any director or officer who shall pay, or declare, or aid in paying or declaring, any dividend, or creating any mortgage or pledge prohibited by this act, or who shall offend against the provisions of the sixth section thereof, shall be punished by imprisonment not exceeding two years, and by fine not exceeding $5,000.

---

## MINORITY REPORT.

I concur in the facts and figures presented in this report, so far as the same could be ascertained through the testimony of those who have been connected with the Union Pacific and Credit Mobilier Companies, and the legal remedies recommended by the committee; but I object to the adoption of the report as incomplete, under the resolution referred to this committee January 6, 1873, until some recommendation is embodied in the same in reference to certain members of Congress who have had transactions with Hon. Oakes Ames, as will be found detailed in the report of Hon. Luke P. Poland, as chairman, &c., believing that the same should be promptly considered and disposed of without further 's of time.

THOS. SWANN.

# CREDIT MOBILIER AND UNION PACIFIC RAILROAD.

---

WASHINGTON, D. C., *January* 10, 1873.

The committee met at 10 a. m. Present: JEREMIAH M. WILSON, of Indiana, chairman; GEORGE F. HOAR, of Massachusetts; THOMAS SWANN, of Maryland; HENRY W. SLOCUM, of New York.

On motion, it was ordered that the chairman be authorized to conduct the examination of witnesses.

Ordered, that this committee will regard the action of the House directing the committee of which Hon. Mr. Poland is chairman to sit with open doors, as an instruction to this committee in this investigation.

Ordered, that the chairman be requested to confer with counsel appointed or to be appointed under resolution of the House of January 6, to ascertain whether aid can be rendered by them to the committee in this investigation.

JOHN B. ALLEY sworn, and examined as follows:

By the CHAIRMAN:

Question. Do you know of the existence of an organization or association, or corporation, by the name of the Credit Mobilier of America?—Answer. I do.

Q. Are you now, or have you at any time been, in any way connected with it? If so, when did your connection with it begin, and in what capacity were you connected with it?—A. I commenced as a stockholder in August, 1865. In May, 1867, I was elected a director. I continued a director, I think, till May, 1869 or 1870; probably May, 1870.

Q. Are you connected with it in any way now?—A. I am simply a stockholder now.

Q. Are you an officer of that organization at this time?—A. I am not.

Q. Have you been connected with it in any other way than you have stated at any time; if so, when?—A. Only as a stockholder and director.

Q. Is this a corporation, or what is the character of the organization?—A. It is a corporation existing in the State of Pennsylvania.

Q. Upon what authority is this corporation organized? Give a history of its organization; the date of its organization; and if it ever had any other name state what it was.—A. This organization was formed under a charter originally from the State of Pennsylvania, in 1859, which was called the Fiscal Agency of the State of Pennsylvania. That is my impression of its original title. After two or three years, it having done nothing, I believe, under the old organization, it was procured by owners and managers of the Union Pacific Railroad Company, wh tended it to be a contracting company for the building of the Pacific Railroad, as I understood. Then its name was changed from the Pennsylvania Fiscal Agency to that of the Credit Mobilier of America. I do not remember exactly at what time; probably in 1863.

Q. Who were the officers of the Union Pacific Railroad Company who procured that charter or transfer?—A. I think the manager was the then vice-president of the Union Pacific Railroad Company, Thomas C. Durant, of New York; John A. Dix was president at that time.

Q. Were there any other officers of the Union Pacific Railroad Company connected with that transaction at that time?—A. I could not say about that; I suppose that Mr. Durant was the man who procured that charter, and, as I understood it, it was procured for the purpose of building this road.

Q. Are there any books or papers showing the character of that transaction and the persons connected with it in existence; and, if so, where may they be found?—A. There are, I suppose; Oliver W. Barnes was the secretary of the Credit Mobilier; he was a resident of Philadelphia then.

Q. Are these books or papers a part of the books and papers of the Credit Mobilier, and are they now in the custody of the officers of that corporation?—A. I presume they are; I said Mr. Barnes was secretary; I think, perhaps, he was the treasurer; he was, as I understood, in those early times of the organization of this company the principal man that I knew anything about.

Q. Can you now give the names of the persons who were parties to the original organization of this Credit Mobilier?—A. Thomas C. Durant was president; Henry C. Crane, of New York, was assistant treasurer, and I think Oliver W. Barnes was the treasurer. Who the secretary was I do not know, and who the other parties at that time in control were I do not remember, if I ever knew.

Q. Was this association organized upon articles of association signed by the persons engaged in this enterprise, and were their stock-books opened?—A. Yes; it was a regular corporation and had very good powers as a corporation; it was procured by these parties as an agency to build the Pacific Railroad. They regarded it as utterly impossible to build the road under the bill which was given them by Congress, except through the intervention of a contracting company or a corporation like this; they took this corporation for that purpose, as I understood, merely as a contracting company.

Q. Where has the business office of the Credit Mobilier been kept since its organization?—A. They had what is called a New York agency, or bureau, which did the business principally, although it was a Pennsylvania corporation. They had a right under authority which was given them by the Pennsylvania legislature to establish an agency or bureau, as they called it, in New York, which they did, and their business was transacted chiefly there.

Q. Have you with you any printed or written copies of any papers to which reference has been made in your testimony?—A. No, sir; I have not.

Q. Was the office or business place of this company ever transferred or removed to the city of Boston?—A. No, sir.

Q. Where was this office in the city of New York?—A. Most of the time, I believe, it was 20 Nassau street.

Q. Where was the office of the Union Pacific Railroad Company?—A. That was in the same building—the same block.

Q. Were these two offices kept in the same room?—A. I think not.

Q. When that contract was made, who were the principal men of interest in, and controlling, the Union Pacific Railroad?—A. The principal stockholders at that time I could not now give. Mr. Durant and General Dix were among them. Not more than two or three hundred thousand dollars had been paid in, and that was a percentage on the shares taken. The first contract for the construction of the Union Pacific Railroad was made, I think, by a Mr. Hoxie, and transferred to the Credit Mobilier. The original parties to the contract had broken down. They had gone on for a while, but had concluded they would rather lose what they had put in than go on. Then they came to Boston, and got Mr. Ames to go into it. But it was determined that the only safe basis to go on with it was through the medium of a contracting company, and they procured the Credit Mobilier for that purpose. My subscription was to the Credit Mobilier, originally, for 500 shares.

By Mr. SLOCUM:

Q. The contract for 247 miles of road, then, was practically with the Credit Mobilier?—A. Practically it was.

Q. The subsequent contracts for building the Union Pacific Railroad were made directly with the Credit Mobilier?—A. No, sir; not at all. The Credit Mobilier never had anything to do with building the road, except the first 247 miles. When I went into the direction of the Credit Mobilier the Hoxie contract had been transferred to it. After that contract was completed, Mr. Durant said the Credit Mobilier should never have another contract while it was under the control of the men who were called the "Ames party," and it never had, except in this way: The Credit Mobilier agreed to guarantee the fulfillment of the Ames contract for a consideration, and furnish money, when called upon, for which they were to have two and a half per cent. commission. When called upon, however, they were unable to furnish the money, and, therefore, they never had really any such connection, and I believe the formal connection ceased a few months afterward.

By Mr. HOAR:

Q. The whole business of the Credit Mobilier consisted in this contract of 247 miles, and their whole property consisted in profits they made on that contract?—A. No; their property consisted, in addition to that in the capital, of $3,750,000, which was paid in money.

By the CHAIRMAN:

Q. Who contracted for building the balance of the road?—A. There were something over 800 miles of the road remaining to be built. Oakes Ames took a contract to build 667 miles, with the privilege of building the balance, if he should conclude to do so. But after the 667 miles were built, under this contract, he declined to take the remainder, and it was built, I understand, for and on account of the stockholders of the Union Pacific Railroad Company. The condition of the contract given to Mr. Ames, and the only condition he would take it upon, was that it should receive the consent of all the stockholders of the Union Pacific Railroad Company at that time.

Q. That portion of the road, then, which Mr. Ames declined to build under the provisions of this contract was built in the interest of the stockholders; by whom was it built; was it a contract let to any one?—A. There was a contract made with a man by the name of Davis; but I think it could not be put through under his contract, and it was finally built for and on account of the Union Pacific Railroad stockholders at that time.

shares of the said company, with all the rights and subject only to such liabilities as other shareholders are subject to; which liabilities are no more than for the payment to the company of the sums due or to become due on the shares held by them; and when new subscriptions are made, the shares may be issued at par or sold for the benefit of the holders of the shares heretofore issued.

SEC. 4. That the by-laws shall prescribe the manner in which the officers and agents of the company shall be chosen, and designate their powers and duties, and their terms of service and compensation; and the principal office of the company shall be in Philadelphia, but the directors, under such rules and regulations as they may prescribe, may establish branches and agencies in Europe and elsewhere, and may deal in exchange, foreign and domestic; but the said company shall not exercise the privilege of banking, nor issue their own notes or bills to be used as bank-notes or as currency.

SEC. 5. That three-fifths of the directors of the said company shall be citizens of the United States, and the majority of the whole shall reside in this State.

SEC. 6. That the said company shall pay to the State treasurer, for the use of the State, a bonus of one-half of one per centum on the sum requisite to be paid in previous to the organization, payable in four equal annual installments, the first payment to be made in one year after the payment on the capital stock shall be made, and also a like bonus on all subsequent payments on account of the capital stock of the said company, or any increase thereof, payable in like manner; and, in addition to such bonus, shall pay such tax upon dividends exceeding six per centum per annum as is or may be imposed by law.

W. C. A. LAWRENCE,
*Speaker of the House of Representatives.*
JNO. CRESWELL, JR.,
*Speaker of the Senate.*

Approved the first day of November, anno Domini one thousand eight hundred and fifty-nine.

WM. F. PACKER.

OFFICE OF THE SECRETARY OF THE COMMONWEALTH,
*Harrisburgh, November* 1, A. D. 1859.

I do hereby certify that the foregoing is a full, true, and correct copy of the original act of the general assembly, as the same remains on file in this office.

In testimony whereof, I have hereunto set my hand and caused the seal of the secretary's office to be affixed, the day and year above written.

WM. M. HIESTER,
*Secretary of the Commonwealth.*

PENNSYLVANIA, *ss:*
[Seal of secretary's office, Pennsylvania.]

---

## LETTERS-PATENT SIGNED BY THE GOVERNOR OF PENNSYLVANIA.

PENNSYLVANIA, *ss:*
A. G. CURTIN.
[L. S.]

In the name and by the authority of the Commonwealth of Pennsylvania, Andrew G. Curtin, governor of the said Commonwealth,

To all whom these presents shall come, sends greeting:

Whereas an act of the general assembly of this Commonwealth, entitled "An act to incorporate the Pennsylvania Fiscal Agency," approved the 1st day of November, A. D. 1859, provides for the organization of a company by the name, style, and title of "The Pennsylvania Fiscal Agency;"

And whereas the commissioners, in accordance with said act of the general assembly, have made application to me for the issuing of letters-patent to said company; and whereas the stipulations and things in the said act directed to be performed have in all respects been fully complied with: Now, know ye, that in pursuance of the power and authority to me given by law, I, Andrew G. Curtin, governor of the said Commonwealth, do, by these presents, which I have caused to be made patent and sealed with the great seal of the State, create and erect the subscribers to the stock of the said company for the number of shares by them subscribed, viz:

Samuel T. Billmeyer, four shares,
liver W. Barnes, two thousand four hundred and ninety-six shares,
arles M. Hall, two thousand four hundred and ninety-five shares,
Reed Myer, five shares,
lane Williams, three shares,

Q. When was the corporation, the Credit Mobilier of America, organized under that charter?—A. This book shows that the first meeting was on the 29th of May, 1863. That was a meeting of the stockholders of the Pennsylvania Fiscal Agency. It was originally the Pennsylvania Fiscal Agency, as the charter shows.

Q. Does that book show the organization of the corporation now known as the Credit Mobilier?—A. Yes, sir.

Q. Who were the original stockholders of the Credit Mobilier, and what amount of stock did each one subscribe for?—A. Charles M. Hall, 2,421 shares of $100 each; Oliver W. Barnes, 2,420 shares of $100 each. There were three or four other parties who had small amounts of stock. I cannot give the names. It was long before I had anything to do with the organization.

Q. Are there any books or papers in your possession that will show who the original stockholders were?—A. No, sir.

Q. Has there ever been any such book, of which you have any knowledge?—A. Not that I know of. There may have been.

Q. Have any books or papers of that corporation been lost, destroyed, or carried away since you have been connected with it?—A. Some of them have been lost.

Q. Do you know what books were lost?—A. The transfer-books were lost—the transfers of stock.

Q. Any others?—A. I do not know of any others.

Q. When were those transfer-books lost?—A. They were last in my possession in December, 1868.

Q. What became of them then?—A. That is more than I can tell.

Q. How did they get out of your possession?—A. At that time I resigned my position as assistant secretary.

Q. When were you re-elected?—A. In May, 1870.

Q. Were those transfer-books among the books of the company at the time you went out of office?—A. Yes; there were two of them—two transfer-books.

Q. And they were not there when you came into office again?—A. No, sir.

Q. Who held that position during the time you were out of office?—A. There was no assistant secretary during that time.

Q. Who was the officer that had possession of those books during that time?—A. They were around in different places. They were part of the time in Philadelphia, and part of the time elsewhere.

Q. What do you mean by "elsewhere?"—A. They were sometimes in New Jersey and sometimes in Philadelphia.

Q. Who was carrying them about in that way?—A. They were [illegible] being carried about; they were put away in various places. [illegible] lon, as president of the Credit Mobilier, ordered them put [illegible]

Q. Put away where?—A. Put away in different places [illegible] know where; I did not go with them. I surrendered [illegible] lon; he took the safe, containing the books and all, and [illegible]

Q. Do you know anything about the purpose for [illegible] carried away?—A. To avoid process in the James Fisk [illegible]

Q. Do you know where Dillon took them when [illegible] away?—A. No, sir; I do not.

Q. You never saw them since?—A. I do not know [illegible] transfer-books away. I do not know that they [illegible] cause it was necessary for me to use some of th[illegible] these books may have been left in the office of [illegible] *road Company*, and lost there during the time t[illegible]

There was a time that I kept out of New York on account of the s Fisk suit, and remained at my home in New Jersey for months.
And you know nothing of these transfer-books since you went out ice?—A. No, sir.
How long before you went out of office had you seen them?—A. I cannot say. These things are three or four years old, and are resh on my memory.
Had you frequent occasion to use these transfer-books?—A. No, I very seldom used them. There was very little transfer of stock.
You have no other means of knowing who were stockholders?—A. stock-ledger shows who were stockholders.
Where is that stock-ledger?—A. Here. The transfer-books were account to anybody. It is possible that I may be able to tell from e of these other books who the original parties were. (Turning to page.) Here they are given:

h for capital stock, $26,645; D. R. Porter, 320 shares; S. T. Billmeyer, 4 shares; W. Barnes, 2,496 shares; Charles M. Hall, 2,495 shares; E. R. Meyer, 5 shares; illiams, 3 shares; E. Williams, 3 shares; S. L. Clement, 3 shares.

hese are all of the original stockholders.
What is the date of that subscription?—A. May 29, 1863, this seems to have been received.
Have you any books that will show who have since become stockholders?—A. Yes, sir; the stock-ledger will show.
We want to know all who have been stockholders at any time the first organization of the Credit Mobilier down to the present—A. I will furnish you with a written list.
r. HOAR. Furnish a list of all persons who have held stock, the ber of shares held by each, the dates, and all the sums paid on unt of stock, with all sums of money or other property divided or ted to each.—A. The last question is one I cannot answer, because I nothing to do with the books.
State whether you were ever a stockholder in the Credit Mobilier pany yourself.—A. Yes, sir.
Are you interested in that stock now?—A. My son holds three shares; is held in trust for him by R. D. Bush, trustee.
When did he procure that?—A. He procured it in 1868 or 1869, not say which.
And you have no interest in the stock of Credit Mobilier except that?—A. No, sir.
How old is your son?—A. Seven years old.
Who furnished the money with which to pay for that stock?—A. mother did.
Out of her separate means?—A. Out of her separate means which ad before I married her.
State to the best of your knowledge what sum of money has been over to that trustee on account of those three shares.—A. I can state by purchases and sales of the Union Pacific stock there has been or $800 realized on these three shares; but then there have been or three purchases and sales of stock. [illegible] been bought by t 20 and sold at 40, and repurchased [illegible]
Why did you do this [illegible] in trust by body else?—A. Because [illegible] Bush it as trustee, and I manage [illegible]
Did you receive the divid[illegible]
Or the allotments?—A. [illegible]
Who did receive them?—[illegible]

Pohl, jr., Charles M. Ghriskey, Thomas Roland, Sidney Dillon, John B. Alley, and Roland G. Hazzard.

Q. Who were the officers?—A. Sidney Dillon president, and Oliver W. Barnes secretary and treasurer.

Q. When was the next election of directors?—A. May 21, 1870.

Q. Who were elected directors then?—A. R. G. Hazzard, Sidney Dillon, Paul Pohl, jr., Charles M. Ghriskey, Thomas Roland, Francis H. Janvier, and B. F. Ham.

Q. Who were the officers?—A. Francis H. Janvier was elected secretary and Sidney Dillon president.

Q. When was the next election?—A. I think that that election in 1870 was the last.

Q. Did this corporation at any time engage in the construction of the Union Pacific Railway?—A. It had charge of building the road to the hundredth meridian.

Q. When did it first engage in that work?—A. Those other witnesses who had charge of it can tell you more definitely than I can.

Q. Is there any entry on the books that will show when the Credit Mobilier engaged first in the construction of the Union Pacific Railway?—A. The Credit Mobilier advanced money to it, and I can show you when that first took place, but I am not familiar with the workings of it, as it was done before I had anything to do with the concern. The Credit Mobilier never built any of the Union Pacific Railroad after I became an officer. The company paid, on account of construction under the Hoxie contract, on March 20, 1865, $202,770. That was the first payment.

Q. On what kind of contract or arrangement did the Credit Mobilier advance money to the Union Pacific Railway Company?—A. I do not know that it did advance any money to the Union Pacific Railway Company, except to lend it the same as to any one else. If the Credit Mobilier Company had any money it did not need, it would lend it.

Q. Have you any paper or memorandum showing the nature of those loans and what kind of obligation was given by the Union Pacific Railway Company, or any one else?—A. There were no obligations given at all. It was nothing but a book account. If the Credit Mobilier lent any money to the Union Pacific Railway Company, it was simply on book account.

Q. There was no note?—A. No note and no obligation.

Q. Or acceptance of any kind?—A. No, sir; and no securities, if it lent the Union Pacific Company any money.

Q. Have you the Hoxie contract here?—A. No, sir; I have not.

Q. Was that contract ever transferred to the Credit Mobilier?—A. It was transferred by the failure of Mr. Hoxie to execute it.

Q. Where is that contract?—A. In New York.

Q. Why did you not bring that with you?—A. I did not understand that you wanted it.

Q. Can you produce a copy of the Hoxie contract?—A. Yes, sir.

Mr. DURANT. Copies of all the contracts are here.

Q. Do you know why that Hoxie contract was assigned to the Credit Mobilier?—A. I do not; I suppose it was because Hoxie failed to carry it out and the Credit Mobilier took it.

Q. Do you know anything of a contract entered into by Oakes Ames with the Union Pacific Company for the construction of the road?—A. Yes, sir.

Q. Have you copies of that contract here?—A. No, sir; I have one in my possession.

property that $47,000,000 was made up of?—A. On 150 miles of the road which was built over the Rocky Mountains, we got $48,000 a mile in Government bonds, and $48,000 in first mortgage bonds; from the termination of the Hoxie contract to the Rocky Mountains we were paid at the rate of $16,000 per mile in Government bonds, and $16,000 a mile in stock. What the bonds did not pay for we took in stock at par.

Q. But the amount of each you are unable to state?—A. I am, but it can be calculated in figures. After we passed the 150 miles, for which we got $48,000 a mile in Government bonds and $48,000 in first mortgage bonds, we received for the rest of the way $32,000 a mile in Government bonds and $32,000 in stock and first mortgage bonds.

Q. Were there any other contracts for constructing the road except those you have named, the Hoxie contract and the Oakes Ames contract?—A. Yes, sir.

Q. In which the Credit Mobilier had an interest?—A. No, sir; none others.

Q. What other contract was there?—A. At the end of my contract there were two contracts made to finish the work to Salt Lake; one the Davis contract, and one the Boomer contract.

Q. Those were persons whom you had no connection with?—A. Yes, sir.

Q. Do you know how much was paid on those contracts?—A. No, sir; but it is my impression that the contractors lost money, although it did not cost nearly as much as the work we did.

Q. Whom do you mean by we?—A. We, the people who carried out the Oakes Ames contract.

Q. I was asking about the Boomer contract and the Davis contract.—A. The Boomer and Davis contracts were assigned to the same trustees as the Oakes Ames contract was assigned to.

Q. You are unable to state how much in cash was paid under those contracts?—A. I cannot tell you, but I believe those contracts were given up by the parties and the work finished by the trustees as trustees.

Q. Can you tell the entire amount which the construction of the Union Pacific Railroad has cost the Union Pacific Railroad Company, including the equipment and the entire paraphernalia of the road?—A. I think about $60,000,000; that is my impression.

Q. That is an average of how much per mile?—A. Between $50,000 and $60,000 per mile. The length of the road is about ten hundred and fifty miles.

Q. Of which amount the company has received about $50,000,000 from the two classes of bonds?—A. Yes.

Q. How much of the stock was actually paid in in cash?—A. It was all paid in cash, or on account of construction, which is the same thing.

Q. What is the amount of the capital stock of the Union Pacific Railroad Company?—A. I think about $36,000,000.

Q. So that, if the company received $50,000,000 from the two cl of bonds and $36,000,000 in cash from the stock, that would $86,000,000 which it had received, besides the land, against an e $60,000,000?—A. That is my impression.

Q. So that, in other words, the company would have $26,000. show for its capital stock besides the lands which the G[illegible] conveyed to it or is hereafter to convey to it?—A. Y[illegible]

Q. State to the committee, as near as you can, w[illegible] by the contractor on each of those contracts.—A. [illegible] property that $47,000,000 was made up of?—A. On 150 miles of the road which was built over the Rocky Mountains, we got $48,000 a mile in Government bonds, and $48,000 in first mortgage bonds; from the termination of the Hoxie contract to the Rocky Mountains we were paid at the rate of $16,000 per mile in Government bonds, and $16,000 a mile in stock. What the bonds did not pay for we took in stock at par.

Q. But the amount of each you are unable to state?—A. I am, but it can be calculated in figures. After we passed the 150 miles, for which we got $48,000 a mile in Government bonds and $48,000 in first mortgage bonds, we received for the rest of the way $32,000 a mile in Government bonds and $32,000 in stock and first mortgage bonds.

Q. Were there any other contracts for constructing the road except those you have named, the Hoxie contract and the Oakes Ames contract?—A. Yes, sir.

Q. In which the Credit Mobilier had an interest?—A. No, sir; none others.

Q. What other contract was there?—A. At the end of my contract there were two contracts made to finish the work to Salt Lake; one the Davis contract, and one the Boomer contract.

Q. Those were persons whom you had no connection with?—A. Yes, sir.

Q. Do you know how much was paid on those contracts?—A. No, sir; but it is my impression that the contractors lost money, although it did not cost nearly as much as the work we did.

Q. Whom do you mean by we?—A. We, the people who carried out the Oakes Ames contract.

Q. I was asking about the Boomer contract and the Davis contract.—A. The Boomer and Davis contracts were assigned to the same trustees as the Oakes Ames contract was assigned to.

Q. You are unable to state how much in cash was paid under those contracts?—A. I cannot tell you, but I believe those contracts were given up by the parties and the work finished by the trustees as trustees.

Q. Can you tell the entire amount which the construction of the Union Pacific Railroad has cost the Union Pacific Railroad Company, including the equipment and the entire paraphernalia of the road?—A. I think about $60,000,000; that is my impression.

Q. That is an average of how much per mile?—A. Between $50,000 and $60,000 per mile. The length of the road is about ten hundred and fifty miles.

Q. Of which amount the company has received about $50,000,000 from the two classes of bonds?—A. Yes.

Q. How much of the stock was actually paid in in cash?—A. It was all paid in cash, or on account of construction, which is the same thing.

Q. What is the amount of the capital stock of the Union Pacific Railroad Company?—A. I think about $36,000,000.

Q. So that, if the company received $50,000,000 from the two classes of bonds and $36,000,000 in cash from the stock, that would make $86,000,000 which it had received, besides the land, against an expense of $60,000,000?—A. That is my impression.

Q. So that, in other words, the company would have $26,000,000 to show for its capital stock besides the lands which the Government has conveyed to it or is hereafter to convey to it?—A. Yes.

Q. State to the committee, as near as you can, what profit was made by the contractor on each of those contracts.—A. That I cannot tell you.

Q. I want to get at the estimates of the engineer?—A. I cannot tell you what the estimates were.

Q. Would you go into a contract of some forty millions of dollars without knowing how you stood?—A. I suppose I knew at the time. But I cannot recollect the estimates now. I estimated that I should make 20 per cent.

Q. I want to know the engineer's estimates?—A. Take 20 per cent. from that and the engineer's estimate would be about $37,000,000.

Q. Have you in your possession now the report of the engineer?—A. I examined it in the office of the Union Pacific Railroad Company.

Q. Can you produce that paper?—A. I do not know whether I can or not.

Q. It would be very satisfactory to the committee if you could produce it, because it is the only way we can estimate the profit which you have derived from the contract. What I want to know is the estimate of the engineer of the cost per mile of the construction of that road.—A. It would vary all the time. I will try to find it.

Q. Do you recollect having ever said that it was not the profits which you expected to derive from the construction of this road that influenced you, but that it was from a motive of patriotism that you threw your self into the field to engineer and carry out this great enterprise?—A. I never thought that, and I do not think I ever said it. Did you ever hear me?

Q. No, sir: I ask you the question.—A. I do not think I ever said it.

By the CHAIRMAN:

Q. I understood you to say that the profits of the Credit Mobilier were about 300 per cent. in dividends.—A. Yes, sir, on that $3,750,000. It will depend on what we get for the stock. I have held my stock. I want to see the road through and to keep the control of it until I get it right. If the stock falls during the month as it has gone down for some days past the dividends would not amount to much.

Q. By your influence and power as a capitalist in the community in which you move how much money do you suppose you raised for the construction of the road?—A. I cannot tell you. I got a good many people to go in by my influence and by guaranteeing them against loss. I took a large amount of stock myself alone and some in connection with others. My brother took a large amount.

Q. Was it your habit to guarantee parties against loss, and did you bring them in in that way?—A. Yes, sir, lots of them.

Q. Did you guarantee those members of Congress who came in?—A. I guaranteed Senator Grimes 10 per cent. on his money. I guaranteed Mr. Adams and I offered to guarantee Mr. Hooper. He thought first that he would take it, and afterward he thought that he would not. I also guaranteed several other parties. People thought I was crazy to make such contracts and to go into such an enterprise. Governor Washburn, of Massachusetts, came to me before I took that contract and offered to loan me $50,000, which they had at the Greenfield Savings Bank. I asked him what security they wanted. He said, "What security can you give?" I mentioned my brother and others. I also gave him $50,000 in stock as collateral. Immediately after that contract he called on me to pay back the loan at a time it was inconvenient to pay it back. He said that the co[…] [ …] thing and that he would not consent that I shoul[d …] that the directors said they would not trust a man [with] such a contract. That is the way the thing was look[ed …]

By Mr. SWANN:

Q. How did you induce these large capitalists to come in?—A. I took them in before I took this large contract.

Q. Were they disposed to "fly the track" when they found that it was not going to be profitable?—A. After we found an easy path over the Rocky Mountains we knew that the contract would be profitable.

Q. Did you not state that it was going to be an immensely profitable contract?—A. The last part of the time I did—after we found this easy grade over the mountains. Previous to that I had my doubts about it. Still I thought it would be a fair investment. I thought it was a good contract to take, and supposed I was going to make 20 per cent. on it. But I cannot carry the data in my mind for half a dozen years. I will try to get you the report of the engineer, if that will satisfy you.

By Mr. HOAR:

Q. How do you reconcile the statement which you made just now that the Credit Mobilier made 300 per cent. on $3,750,000, which would be over $11,000,000, with your answer to me that you thought the entire profit made out of this contract was only about $7,000,000?—A. If I could sit down and figure it up I could get nearer to it. These are round guesses.

Mr. HOAR. I thought that that was something of a discrepancy even for round guesses.

The WITNESS. I suppose there would be some profit out of the Hoxie contract; I do not know.

Q. What is your present judgment?—A. My present judgment is that we made some $8,000,000 or $9,000,000 on the Oakes Ames contract.

Q. The Credit Mobilier profit alone would have amounted to over $11,000,000 if they made 300 per cent.?—A. Part of it came out of Credit Mobilier stock, which is not now worth 25 cents on the dollar. Its capital has been worked up on these contracts.

Q. Do you mean that, in addition to the original par value of the stock, there was a profit of over $11,000,000, or do you mean that the stock became worth 300 per cent., which would make a profit of 200 per cent?—A. I think the profit was more than 200 per cent. I think it must have been 300 per cent., but I cannot tell you from memory.

The committee adjourned to 15th January, at half past 10.

---

WASHINGTON, D. C., *January* 15, 1873.

The committee met at half past 10. Present, the chairman, Messrs. Hoar, Shellabarger, Swann, and Slocum.

HENRY C. CRANE sworn and examined.

By the CHAIRMAN:

Question. Where do you reside?—Answer. At Yonkers, Westchester County, New York.

Q. Have you been at any time an officer in the corporation known as the Credit Mobilier of America?—A. From the time of the removal of the company's agency from Philadelphia to New York until May, 1867, I was assistant treasurer. I cannot tell the date that I commenced, but it was after the time it came to New York. I should say it was in 1864.

*Q. Were you then,* and are you now, a stockholder in the Credit trust.—A. That was for relatives of Mr. Hazzard, one of the other stockholders.

Q. Josiah Bardwell appears as the holder of three hundred shares in trust.—A. I do not for whom he held it. I think it was for a Mrs. Nourse, some lady-friend of his.

Q. You are down on this list as the holder of sixty shares in trust.—A. Yes.

Q. For whom was that held?—A. I do not recollect now. I held stock for Mr. Thomas C. Durant in trust, and I held some for Mrs. Clarissa C. Cooke.

Q. Oakes Ames seems to have been the holder of ninety-three shares in trust. Do you know for whom he held them?—A. I do not know anything about it.

Q. On the 17th of June, 1868, as appears by the list of dividends declared on that day, Oakes Ames appears to have been the holder, as trustee, of three hundred and forty-three shares of this Credit Mobilier stock. Do you know from what source he derived those three hundred and forty-three shares?—A. The books will tell. I think that stock was transferred to his name from Mr. Dillon's name.

Q. Please look at the books and see how that stock came into Oakes Ames's hands?—A. He received thirty shares as trustee on 8th January, 1868, from Sidney Dillon, president, and he received on 20th January, 1868, two hundred and twenty shares. These, with the ninety-three shares which he received before, made the three hundred and forty-three shares.

Q. Do you know for whom he held that stock?—A. I do not know anything about it.

Q. Or on what account?—A. I know nothing about it.

By Mr. SHELLABARGER:

Q. Were you then connected with the company?—A. No, sir, I think not. I was in New York in 1867, and this was in May, 1868, in Boston.

By Mr. SWANN:

Q. Do you know whether this stock was purchased in the market and at what rate?—A. I know nothing about it, except that the books will show what he paid for it.

Q. Tell us that.—A. (After examining books.) He paid par and six months' interest at 7 per cent. for these two hundred and fifty additional shares on January 8th and January 30, 1868.

Q. Look and see whether that was not stock that was held by the Credit Mobilier and transferred to him?—A. No, sir, because the transfer shows that it was stock held in the name of Sidney Dillon, which he had received from Thomas C. Durant, and which Mr. Dillon transferred to Mr. Ames. The entry is that the company received from Oakes Ames $3,000 for thirty shares of stock and $105 in interest. There are ten shares on the 31st of January, thirty on the 21st, and one hundred and eighty on the 7th of February, paid for with six months' interest. That makes two hundred and twenty shares. That, with the thirty shares and the ninety-three shares, makes the three hundred and forty-three shares which Mr. Oakes Ames held in trust.

Q. From whom did Anna M. Dodge receive the stock which she holds?—A. The entry of it is: "29th February, 1868, capital stock, Anna M. Dodge, certificate No. 372, for 100 shares." There would be no transfer on that if it is new stock; and from its not having been transferred I should say that *it was new stock*—some that the comp we decided upon and adopted this line of the Black Hills, in the spring of 1867.

Q. Who was the engineer that had charge of that part of the survey which covered the region of the Black Hills?—A. Engineer Evans was really the man entitled to the credit of discovering this pass. My first knowledge of the pass was in the spring of 1867.

Q. And it was reported to be a comparatively easy pass at that time?—A. Yes, sir, a much easier pass than we had anticipated.

Q. What was the character of the survey reported to you by your engineers as having been made at that time? I mean as to the extent of the observations and survey? Was it an instrumental survey or was it mere ocular observations?—A. I know nothing of the details of the survey. I may be mistaken as to the time I learned of this pass. Perhaps it was not so early as I have stated.

Q. Go on with your statement.—A. I had got to where we had sold the bonds, and when we had all found that it was not going to cost us so much to get over the Rocky Mountains as we had anticipated. The result of that was that in the fall of 1867 the Credit Mobilier stock went up first to 160. The first notice that I had of the advance was that some one sold at 160 to 165; and before the next summer it went up still higher.

Q. When was that date?—A. That was in the fall of 1867.

Q. Was the Credit Mobilier stock quoted in the newspapers?—A. No, sir; but I learned of the sale. The first sale that I knew of was a sale by Mr. Alley to Mr. Peter Butler. I understood that it was at 160 or 165. I have learned since this discussion that it was still higher.

Q. You let the contract for building these six hundred and sixty-seven miles west of the hundredth meridian to Oakes Ames?—A. Yes.

Q. You let that on actual surveys and location by your engineer?—A. Yes.

Q. Who was that engineer?—A. The chief engineer, who was really the letting engineer, was General Dodge, but he was not the constructing engineer, nor the engineer on whom I think Mr. Durant relied the most for the work to be done. We had a consulting engineer in New York, Mr. Seymour; a constructing engineer, Mr. Reed, and an assistant engineer, Mr. Evans, who had active charge of the line, and many others. Mr. Durant was very careful about their reports. He did not rely upon General Dodge alone, but he sent out his constructing engineer. I do not think they perfected the route over the Rocky Mountains until late in 1867.

Q. Describe now in what form the reports of the engineers were made to the company prior to the letting of the contract to Mr. Ames. If they included profiles of the road, state that. Describe fully what kind of reports were made and how full and complete they were.—A. I know that the reports were very voluminous.

Q. Did they cover the whole six hundred and sixty-seven miles which Mr. Ames took?—A. That is my impression.

Q. Then they did let the contract on actual surveys, and not on imaginary ones?—A. On actual surveys.

Q. How was that letting conducted? Was there an offer made by the Union Pacific Railroad Company to all the world to come in and take the work at the lowest bid?—A. I do not think there was.

Q. How was it done?—A. I cannot say; it was done during my sickness, which confined me four or five weeks in my home in Connecticut.

Q. Go on with your narrative.—A. We went on with the work with great rapidity, laying two or three miles of track a day, until the year

[illegible]

... of 1862.

Q. What secured the benefits of the [illegible] Railroad Company?—A. Yes, to [illegible] by the other company the privilege of [illegible].

Q. What distance is that from the [illegible]?—A. Somewhat over eight hundred miles.

Q. How far is it from where the [illegible] began?—A. Something over eight hundred [illegible].

Q. How do you explain the difference [illegible] fifteen miles and this eight hundred miles?—A. [illegible] President of the Union Pacific Railroad Company [illegible] should be no delay in driving the work [illegible] the line of the road, with a [illegible] to [illegible]

[illegible]

west of Omaha; but after we got out forty miles from Omaha, the Creator could not have given us a better country to build a line of railroad through, and that continued nearly out to the base of the Rocky Mountains.

Q. What distance is that?—A. 517 miles.

Q. That country was as good as nature could have made it?—A. Yes, sir. It is decomposed granite at the base, which will be for ever just as perfect as can be. We built the road just as perfect as a railroad can be built, and we built it at great rapidity and at an immense cost for everything. The cost of building a road and driving it so fast is almost fabulous; but we saved the extra expense in interest.

Q. Why did that great increase of cost result from the rapidity with which you did the work?—A. It resulted from the immense surplus of help we had to have in doing the work so fast. For instance, you had a thousand men to lay the track. If there was any little delay in procuring the materials these thousand men were idle, and so in every other department.

Q. You have got now to the foot of the Rocky Mountains; how near was that to the western end of the 667 miles of the Oakes Ames contract?—A. About half way.

Q. Describe the road from that onward?—A. The road from that over the Rocky Mountains was nothing like as expensive as we expected it to be, although it was very expensive through the granite of the Rocky Mountains and up a road of 80 to 90 feet to the mile and circuitous. Then there was the bridge over Dale Creek, a chasm of 600 or 700 feet and 130 feet high. We had to get all the materials out there ahead of the road, and it cost ten times as much to build that bridge as it would cost now. And so down the mountains beyond the Dale Creek bridge it was solid rock all the way through till we got to Laramie plains. From the Laramie plains till the valley of the Green River was comparatively an easy road to build. One mistake was that an old Government director, Jesse L. Williams, a very nice man, and Mr. Brinkerhofer, another nice man, insisted upon our making a cut through every rising in the Laramie plains, which probably cost us millions of dollars, as we had afterwards to fill up these cuts. I was satisfied at the time that it was a great mistake, but they thought otherwise. Then we came to the Green River, which was a very costly and expensive place to build a road and we came out to the Carbon and got to the coal-fields, and down Butte Creek, where it was impossible for the cattle to drink the water without dying. There was no vegetation there. Every particle of corn and hay and grain for the cattle, and food for the men, had to be carried ahead 200 or 300 miles, where the men were doing the grading. A pound of corn, brought there, cost perhaps twenty times as much as it cost where it started from. All this made the construction mighty expensive. If we could have waited to complete the road till 1876, I think we could have built the road at less than half of what it actually cost us; but then, on the other hand, the interest account would have ruined us. We built the road seven years inside of our time.

Q. When was the road completed?—A. On the 10th of May, 1869, more than seven years inside of the time allowed. One of the incidental advantages from the early finishing of the road has been that over twelve millions worth of silver has been brought from Salt Lake Valley alone this year, by which the country will profit several times the interest paid on the bonds. This is clean profit to the country, of course. One little lead and silver mine which *I and my associates* bought for $12,000, we sold to *the people of Amsterdam for* $400,000. I give that as

[illegible]

Q. What was the date of [illegible] ... of 1868.

Q. [illegible] secured the benefits of the [illegible] Railroad Company?—A. Yes, to [illegible] of the other company the privilege of [illegible].

Q. What distance is that from the [illegible] somewhat over eight hundred miles. [illegible]

Q. How far is it from [illegible] begin?—A. Something over eight hundred [illegible].

Q. How do you explain the difference [illegible] seven miles and this eight hundred miles?—A. [illegible] President of the Union Pacific Railroad Company [illegible] would be no delay in driving the work [illegible] on the line of the road, with a [illegible] to [illegible].

Q. Mr. Ames's contract then [illegible]

[illegible]

west of Omaha; but after we got out forty miles from Omaha, the Creator could not have given us a better country to build a line of railroad through, and that continued nearly out to the base of the Rocky Mountains.

Q. What distance is that?—A. 517 miles.

Q. That country was as good as nature could have made it?—A. Yes, sir. It is decomposed granite at the base, which will be for ever just as perfect as can be. We built the road just as perfect as a railroad can be built, and we built it at great rapidity and at an immense cost for everything. The cost of building a road and driving it so fast is almost fabulous; but we saved the extra expense in interest.

Q. Why did that great increase of cost result from the rapidity with which you did the work?—A. It resulted from the immense surplus of help we had to have in doing the work so fast. For instance, you had a thousand men to lay the track. If there was any little delay in procuring the materials these thousand men were idle, and so in every other department.

Q. You have got now to the foot of the Rocky Mountains; how near was that to the western end of the 667 miles of the Oakes Ames contract?—A. About half way.

Q. Describe the road from that onward?—A. The road from that over the Rocky Mountains was nothing like as expensive as we expected it to be, although it was very expensive through the granite of the Rocky Mountains and up a road of 80 to 90 feet to the mile and circuitous. Then there was the bridge over Dale Creek, a chasm of 600 or 700 feet and 130 feet high. We had to get all the materials out there ahead of the road, and it cost ten times as much to build that bridge as it would cost now. And so down the mountains beyond the Dale Creek bridge it was solid rock all the way through till we got to Laramie plains. From the Laramie plains till the valley of the Green River was comparatively an easy road to build. One mistake was that an old Government director, Jesse L. Williams, a very nice man, and Mr. Brinkerhofer, another nice man, insisted upon our making a cut through every rising in the Laramie plains, which probably cost us millions of dollars, as we had afterwards to fill up these cuts. I was satisfied at the time that it was a great mistake, but they thought otherwise. Then we came to the Green River, which was a very costly and expensive place to build a road and we came out to the Carbon and got to the coal-fields, and down Butte Creek, where it was impossible for the cattle to drink the water without dying. There was no vegetation there. Every particle of corn and hay and grain for the cattle, and food for the men, had to be carried ahead 200 or 300 miles, where the men were doing the grading. A pound of corn, brought there, cost perhaps twenty times as much as it cost where it started from. All this made the construction mighty expensive. If we could have waited to complete the road till 1876, I think we could have built the road at less than half of what it actually cost us; but then, on the other hand, the interest account would have ruined us. We built the road seven years inside of our time.

Q. When was the road completed?—A. On the 10th of May, 1869, more than seven years inside of the time allowed. One of the incidental advantages from the early finishing of the road has been that over twelve millions worth of silver has been brought from Salt Lake Valley alone this year, by which the country will profit several times the interest paid on the bonds. This is clean profit to the country, of course. One little lead and silver mine which *I and my associates* bought for $12,-000, we sold to *the people of Amsterdam* for $400,000. I give that as

[illegible]

Q. What was the date of that act of Congress? [illegible] summer of 1868.

Q. What secured the benefits of the [illegible] Railroad Company?—A. The [illegible] Promontory [illegible] all the other company the privilege of [illegible] Ogden.

Q. What distance is that from the [illegible]—A. Somewhat over eight hundred miles.

Q. How far is it from where the eastern and [illegible] began?—A. Something over eight hundred miles.

Q. How do you explain the difference between [illegible] miles and this eight hundred miles?—A. [illegible] president of the Union Pacific Railroad Company [illegible] would be no delay in finishing the work [illegible] the line of the road, with a [illegible] there, to continue [illegible]

Q. [illegible] contract [illegible]

[illegible]

west of Omaha; but after we got out forty miles from Omaha, the Creator could not have given us a better country to build a line of railroad through, and that continued nearly out to the base of the Rocky Mountains.

Q. What distance is that?—A. 517 miles.

Q. That country was as good as nature could have made it?—A. Yes, sir. It is decomposed granite at the base, which will be for ever just as perfect as can be. We built the road just as perfect as a railroad can be built, and we built it at great rapidity and at an immense cost for everything. The cost of building a road and driving it so fast is almost fabulous; but we saved the extra expense in interest.

Q. Why did that great increase of cost result from the rapidity with which you did the work?—A. It resulted from the immense surplus of help we had to have in doing the work so fast. For instance, you had a thousand men to lay the track. If there was any little delay in procuring the materials these thousand men were idle, and so in every other department.

Q. You have got now to the foot of the Rocky Mountains; how near was that to the western end of the 667 miles of the Oakes Ames contract?—A. About half way.

Q. Describe the road from that onward?—A. The road from that over the Rocky Mountains was nothing like as expensive as we expected it to be, although it was very expensive through the granite of the Rocky Mountains and up a road of 80 to 90 feet to the mile and circuitous. Then there was the bridge over Dale Creek, a chasm of 600 or 700 feet and 130 feet high. We had to get all the materials out there ahead of the road, and it cost ten times as much to build that bridge as it would cost now. And so down the mountains beyond the Dale Creek bridge it was solid rock all the way through till we got to Laramie plains. From the Laramie plains till the valley of the Green River was comparatively an easy road to build. One mistake was that an old Government director, Jesse L. Williams, a very nice man, and Mr. Brinkerhofer, another nice man, insisted upon our making a cut through every rising in the Laramie plains, which probably cost us millions of dollars, as we had afterwards to fill up these cuts. I was satisfied at the time that it was a great mistake, but they thought otherwise. Then we came to the Green River, which was a very costly and expensive place to build a road and we came out to the Carbon and got to the coal-fields, and down Butte Creek, where it was impossible for the cattle to drink the water without dying. There was no vegetation there. Every particle of corn and hay and grain for the cattle, and food for the men, had to be carried ahead 200 or 300 miles, where the men were doing the grading. A pound of corn, brought there, cost perhaps twenty times as much as it cost where it started from. All this made the construction mighty expensive. If we could have waited to complete the road till 1876, I think we could have built the road at less than half of what it actually cost us; but then, on the other hand, the interest account would have ruined us. We built the road seven years inside of our time.

Q. When was the road completed?—A. On the 10th of May, 1869, more than seven years inside of the time allowed. One of the incidental advantages from the early finishing of the road has been that over twelve millions worth of silver has been brought from Salt Lake Valley alone this year, by which the country will profit several times the interest paid on the bonds. This is clean profit to the country, of course. One little lead and silver mine which *I and my associates* bought for $12,-00, we sold to *the people of Amsterdam for $400,000.* I give that as

west of Omaha; but after we got out forty miles from Omaha, the Creator could not have given us a better country to build a line of railroad through, and that continued nearly out to the base of the Rocky Mountains.

Q. What distance is that?—A. 517 miles.

Q. That country was as good as nature could have made it?—A. Yes, sir. It is decomposed granite at the base, which will be for ever just as perfect as can be. We built the road just as perfect as a railroad can be built, and we built it at great rapidity and at an immense cost for everything. The cost of building a road and driving it so fast is almost fabulous; but we saved the extra expense in interest.

Q. Why did that great increase of cost result from the rapidity with which you did the work?—A. It resulted from the immense surplus of help we had to have in doing the work so fast. For instance, you had a thousand men to lay the track. If there was any little delay in procuring the materials these thousand men were idle, and so in every other department.

Q. You have got now to the foot of the Rocky Mountains; how near was that to the western end of the 667 miles of the Oakes Ames contract?—A. About half way.

Q. Describe the road from that onward?—A. The road from that over the Rocky Mountains was nothing like as expensive as we expected it to be, although it was very expensive through the granite of the Rocky Mountains and up a road of 80 to 90 feet to the mile and circuitous. Then there was the bridge over Dale Creek, a chasm of 600 or 700 feet and 130 feet high. We had to get all the materials out there ahead of the road, and it cost ten times as much to build that bridge as it would cost now. And so down the mountains beyond the Dale Creek bridge it was solid rock all the way through till we got to Laramie plains. From the Laramie plains till the valley of the Green River was comparatively an easy road to build. One mistake was that an old Government director, Jesse L. Williams, a very nice man, and Mr. Brinkerhofer, another nice man, insisted upon our making a cut through every rising in the Laramie plains, which probably cost us millions of dollars, as we had afterwards to fill up these cuts. I was satisfied at the time that it was a great mistake, but they thought otherwise. Then we came to the Green River, which was a very costly and expensive place to build a road and we came out to the Carbon and got to the coal-fields, and down Butte Creek, where it was impossible for the cattle to drink the water without dying. There was no vegetation there. Every particle of corn and hay and grain for the cattle, and food for the men, had to be carried ahead 200 or 300 miles, where the men were doing the grading. A pound of corn, brought there, cost perhaps twenty times as much as it cost where it started from. All this made the construction mighty expensive. If we could have waited to complete the road till 1876, I think we could have built the road at less than half of what it actually cost us; but then, on the other hand, the interest account would have ruined us. We built the road seven years inside of our time.

Q. When was the road completed?—A. On the 10th of May, 1869, more than seven years inside of the time allowed. One of the incidental advantages from the early finishing of the road has been that over twelve millions worth of silver has been brought from Salt Lake Valley alone this year, by which the country will profit several times the interest paid on the bonds. This is clean profit to the country, of course. One little lead and silver mine which *I and my associates* bought for $12,-000, we sold to *the people of Amsterdam* for $400,000. I give that as extending the Hoxie contract to the one hundredth meridian?—A. That resolution of the board was on the 5th of January, 1866. The resolution was to consider the Hoxie contract extended to embrace the fifty-eight miles of road already completed under the Boomer contract.

Q. After that work had been performed under the Boomer contract?—A. Well, the board did not recognize that contract, but the road was built under it.

Q. And after the road had been built for that distance under that Boomer contract, the Hoxie contract was extended over it?—A. Yes.

Q. Was it paid for under the Hoxie contract?—A. No, it was not. I entered a protest and got out an injunction and prevented it.

Adjourned to January 16.

---

WASHINGTON, D. C., *January* 16, 1873.

The committee met at 10 o'clock a. m., all the members present.

Examination of THOMAS C. DURANT continued.

The WITNESS. I find a resolution in the books that the engineer's reports were called for and ordered to be printed.

By the CHAIRMAN:

Q. What reports do you refer to?—A. Engineer's estimates, with the quantities.

Q. Have they been printed?—A. I presume they have been; the board had them before it.

Q. But you have no copy of them here?—A. No, sir.

Q. When the committee adjourned last night you were speaking, I believe, in regard to a resolution of the board to extend the Hoxie contract over the road which had been constructed under the Boomer contract?—A. The Boomer contract was never formally approved by the board.

Q. Have you that resolution of the board?—A. Yes, sir; I have a copy of the resolution here. It was passed on the 5th of January, 1867.

Q. Please read that resolution.—A. "*Resolved*, That the Union Pacific Railroad Company will and do hereby consider the Hoxie contract extended to the point already completed, namely, 305 miles from Omaha, and that the officers of this company are hereby authorized to settle with the Credit Mobilier at $50,000 a mile for the additional fifty-eight miles.

"The yeas and nays being had on agreeing to the resolution, it was adopted by the following vote:

"Yeas: Messrs. Bushnell, Tuttle, McComb, Lamport, Ames, Duffy, Dillon, and Carter.

"Nays: Messrs. Harbaugh, Ashmun, Sherman, and Williams."

Q. Which of those men were Government directors?—A. Carter, a Government director, voted in the affirmative.

Q. Which of those voting in the negative were Government directors?—A. All of them.

Q. What had been the cost of the construction of the road over which the Hoxie contract was to be extended?—A. About $20,000 a mile, exclusive of equipment. I see the resolution of the board calls for equipment to the amount of $7,500 a mile.

Q. Then the cost of construction of this piece of road was $27,500 per mile?—A. About *that*.

I do not know that my protest is on the books of the company, for the board subsequently passed a resolution expunging my protest, and ordered to be written across it, in red ink, "expunged by order of the board."

Q. What was the next thing done in furtherance of the construction of this road ?—A. There were committees appointed to get estimates of the heavy work, &c.

Q. State who was the engineer of the company at the time the work was done under the Boomer contract.—A. That Boomer contract was known on the books of the company as the Gessner contract. Mr. Gessner was appointed as agent by Boomer, and Boomer afterward sold it to him.

Q. Who was the chief engineer at the time that that fifty-eight miles was constructed ?—A. I think that at that time each division had its engineer in charge. I am not positive whether it was Mr. Evans who was engineer of that division. We had some ten or fifteen engineers on the different divisions.

By Mr. SWANN:

Q. Were the reports of those resident engineers on the different sections indorsed by the chief engineer before being submitted to the company ?—A. They were not at first, because, instead of a chief engineer we kept a consulting engineer, and the work extended over so large sections of country that we had the reports made direct to the office. Subsequently the chief engineer became a member of Congress, and it took too long to get things round. The reports were generally submitted to him and he signed them.

Q. Did he sanction them ?—A. He sanctioned all the reports on which payments were made. I think that most of the reports were submitted to him.

Q. And they came in as the reports of the chief engineer ?—A. We made, at first, each man chief of his own division. We thought two hundred or two hundred and fifty miles was about as much as any engineer could attend to.

Q. What I want to know is, whether the chief engineer was responsible for the reports ?—A. Yes; he was responsible to the company.

Q. And no disbursements were made except under the order of the chief engineer ?—A. They were made on his estimates. I suppose his subs made them up and had them sent.

Q. You are not able at present to give the name of the chief engineer ?—A. I am not positive whether General Dodge was then chief engineer or not.

Q. Was General Dodge then a member of Congress ?—A. No; he was elected afterward.

Q. How long afterward ?—A. I do not recollect.

By the CHAIRMAN:

Q. In regard to this Hoxie contract I find that it contains a provision that the Union Pacific Railroad Company was to pay for work done under it at the rate of $50,000 for every mile completed. Explain in what way, if any, the company would have been wronged by the extension of the Hoxie contract over this fifty-eight miles.—A. The Hoxie contract was made (with no one interested in it) as a *bona-fide* contract. The parties who became subsequently interested in the Hoxie c
and in the Credit Mobilier, became directors of the Union Paci
road Company; and then, to extend that contract over a piec

practicability. We simply found we had an elevation we could run a railroad over; that was what we were trying to get at.

Q. What was the difference in the estimates of the two roads?—A. I never read the estimates. I never figured the estimates of that route, as it was reported impracticable by the Secretary of War at the time.

Q. What is your opinion of the amount that Mr. Ames netted in his individual capacity by the approval of this contract?—A. I can give you that from the book.

Q. Can you not give it in round numbers?—A. No, I cannot. I would not recollect it if I heard it a dozen times.

Q. You cannot say whether it was five, four, or three millions?—A. No, sir.

By the CHAIRMAN:

Q. I will ask you if you know of any moneys that this railroad or the Credit Mobilier have used, either directly or indirectly, for the purpose of influencing or procuring the election of any person to the United States Senate?—A. I do not.

Q. Do you know of any person connected with either of those corporations, at any time using money or furnishing money for that purpose?—A. Not of the company's money.

Q. Anybody's money?—A. I have furnished money for the elections myself.

Q. When did you furnish it?—A. That was my own money.

Q. I am going to examine further about that. I want to know when you furnished that money.—A. I have furnished money a good many times for elections.

Q. I am speaking of elections of Senators. How many times have you furnished money for that purpose?—A. I pay very little attention to politics. I do not know whether it was for Senators' election or not. I gave a check some five or six years ago to be sent to Senator Harlan. It was sent to some committee, but what it was for I do not know.

Q. That was pending the senatorial contest there?—A. I do not know. Some of our parties were mixing up in politics, and I was very much annoyed at the time. I refused to do anything at first, but afterward furnished them money.

Q. For what purpose did you furnish that money?—A. I could not tell you, for I even forget the committees whom I sent it to. Mr. Harlan once said to me, "Are you never going to help us in our election?" I said, "When you cannot do anything, I will do what I can."

Q. What did you furnish?—A. I gave two checks on different occasions, for $5,000 each, but it has been called to my mind by Mr. Crane that one was a subscription to some Methodist institution, and I believe now it was something of that kind.

Mr. CRANE. A Methodist college.

The WITNESS. Perhaps so.

Q. You furnished $5,000?—A. Yes, sir; and probably $10,000. There was no concealment at all. I told the young men to send the check to Senator Harlan's order. I do not know but what he was chairman of a committee.

Q. I want you to give me, as nearly as you can, the date of those transactions.—A. It was 1865 or 1866; it was a year or two subsequent to the passage of the act.

Q. Was Mr. Harlan at that time Secretary of the Interior?—A. I do not recollect whether he was or not.

Q. Do you recollect whether at the time you gave those checks he was that these subdivisions begin at the eastern end, in the order of their statement in the contract?—A. The Government engineer established the base at the foot of the Rocky Mountains, which is the basis for the $48,000 per mile. One hundred and fifty miles west of that point the $32,000 per mile commenced, and that continued through the Ames contract.

Q. I see a stipulation here that the seven trustees in the assignment of the contract were to receive for their services as trustees a reasonable compensation, not to exceed the sum of $3,000 per annum; what did they in fact receive?—A. They received $3,000 per annum. That was paid for one or two years, and I believe they have received nothing since.

Q. For one or two years they received that, and the residue is still unpaid?—A. Yes, sir.

By Mr. HOAR:

Q. Suppose this road had been completed economically, and without unusual haste, and the capital subscribed had been paid in cash, would not the amount of the Government loan of $27,000,000, and the capital stock of $36,000,000, amounting together to $63,000,000, have completed and equipped the road, without reference to the land-grants?—A. Hardly, at the time they commenced work.

Q. Would it not have substantially?—A. With the facilities as they were then, I doubt whether it would have.

Q. In your opinion did the construction and equipment of that road cost the persons who furnished both more than that amount, $63,000,000? I include in that the payment of land damages.—A. I think $65,000,000 would have covered it.

Q. In that case, then, the expenditure of the Government loan of $27,000,000, the capital stock of $36,000,000, and $2,000,000 more in cash, would have completed the entire road and equipped it without reference to the land-grant. Now, if that has been done, would not the stockholders now have had the entire road and its equipment, subject only to the Government claim of $27,000,000, together with all the land-grants?—A. So far as it was completed, they would.

Q. State now what in your best judgment would be the present value of such property, including the land-grant and all its prospects of future development and increase?—A. I have no idea what the road is earning now.

Q. You were its vice-president for many years?—A. I have not been connected with the road for two years, not even as a stockholder.

Q. Have you not a general knowledge of what the road is earning?—A. No, sir.

Q. Look at this statement of the earnings for eleven months in 1872, and state then what you should think the value of such property to be?—A. I should think the stock would [illegible] worth 80. T[illegible] earnings would be 6⅔ per cent., but still you [illegible] into [illegible] on the depreciation of property and the r[illegible] even.

Q. Did you take into considera[illegible] pect of [illegible] crease of trade?—A. No, sir.

Q. Have you taken into consid[illegible] the [illegible] land-grants? Your calculation is bas[illegible] earnings alone.

[illegible], have you any doubt, as an [illegible] a correct statement of the [illegible] this land-grant, that the c[illegible] company owning the entire road, equipments, rolling-stock, &c., as they do, subject only to the Government claim of $27,000,000—would be worth considerably above par?—A. No, sir. I do not think it would be worth par. In the first place, I do not think there are two million acres of land worth a cent.

Q. You still think it would be worth 75 or 80?—A. Yes, sir.

Q. What do you think it to be worth now?—A. It depends upon whether the street is "long" or "short" of the stock. I think the last quotation is about 35.

Q. I will ask you the general question whether any of the persons who have held the office of Government director in the Union Pacific Railroad since its original establishment have ever been interested, directly or indirectly, so far as you know, in the Credit Mobilier, or in any contract with the road?—A. I do not recall any, except the case of Mr. Neilson, the son-in-law of James Brooks, about which I have testified.

Q. With that exception, have any of the Government directors been interested in any manner in the Credit Mobilier, or in any contract for the construction of the road?—A. I do not call to mind any.

Q. Or supplying it with coal?—A. No, sir.

Q. I will ask you to read over the list of Government directors and see whether you wish to qualify your answer.—A. I do not recollect any.

Q. Are you a member of the Wyoming Coal Company?—A. I subscribed to its stock to help its organization.

Q. Who are the principal owners of that company?—A. The company was organized for the benefit of the Union Pacific Railroad, and to supply it with coal. Several of the directors subscribed to its stock, as stockholders of the Union Pacific road. The parties who work the mine have [illegible] stock, and the rest is held for the benefit of the [illegible] Railroad.

Q. S[illegible] dividend of the stock of this coal company, is [illegible] the treasury of the company?—A. The company [illegible] $1.82. Any dividend would go to [illegible] $20,000 of stock, which I paid for in in[illegible]. The only reason that it stands in my [illegible] Union Pacific will not release the parties that [illegible] in case of debt. I believe that all the [illegible] about 15 per cent. is held in trust for the Union Pacific road.

By the CHAIRMAN:

Q. W[illegible] the first contract entered into in regard to this Wyoming Coal Company?—A. I think it was in 1868.

Q. Who executed that contract?—A. I do not know; I never saw it [illegible] was executed. I think Mr. Oliver Ames, Mr. Godfrey, and [illegible] Oliver Ames executed it as president of the road.

Q. W[illegible] was the company organized?—A. I presume the date stated [illegible] February 21, 1868.

Q. [illegible] that the Wyoming Coal Company was organized [illegible] this contract I have referred to?—A. Yes, sir.

Q. W[illegible] agreement assigned to the Wyoming Coal Company?—A. [illegible] to have been.

Q. [illegible] what law was the Wyoming Coal Company organized?—A. [illegible] law of the State of Nebraska.

Q. Who were the directors and officers of the coal company?—A. [illegible] think, were John Duff, Mr. Oliver Ames, and Mr. W[illegible] [illegible] remember whether Mr. Bushnell was one or not [illegible] and Mr. Wardell secretary or treasurer.

... loaned to the Credit
...—A. ... of the books.
... was paid to him?—A. I ...
... connected with the Credit M...
... Congress?—A. No, ...
... Railroad Company?—...

... been used by ei...
... with either of the...
... of Congress or

... that sort had been do...
... such purpose.
... been used for the p...
... by the Governm...
... anything else in c...
... Government?—A. I
... heard of it.
... by any person connected

... being paid over by the C...
...—A. No, sir; I do not.
... being employed by the Credit
... appertaining to either of these c...

... of the Union Pacific Railroad Compa...

... of the details of the business?—A. E...
...rsay.
... of the employment of Joseph B. St...
... of that corporation?—A. Only from

... hear anything on that subject?—A. Fro...

... did Mr. Durant give you in relat...
... he had employed him to settle with p...
... lines of railroad, particularly the L...

... gave you that information?—A. F...

... having employed a man named Hay...
... several persons; I do not recollect
...

... money handled by those perso...

... about these men?—A. It wa...

... say in reference to the susp...
... the Railroad Company?—A...
... a discussion about it

... which gave rise to this co...
... casual conversation. It ...
...

... information in reference t...
...—A. No, sir.

By Mr. SHELLABARGER:

Q. If there was such an issuance in gross, that must have been taken up and consolidated, and new issues made to the individual stockholders who became entitled to the dividend?—A. That would have been the correct and usual mode of doing it—to subdivide the certificate and surrender the gross one.

The following are the papers referred to by the witness in his testimony:

CREDIT MOBILIER OF AMERICA, NEW YORK AGENCY,
*20 Nassau street, January 2, 1867.*

——— ———, Esq.

DEAR SIR: At a meeting of the executive committee of the board of directors of this company, held at this agency, on the 28th day of December last, the following resolutions were adopted, viz:

*Resolved*, That in order to equalize the date of payment to increase stock subscription made under agreement of February 26, 1867, interest be allowed to each subscriber from the date of payment to July 1, 1867, at the rate of 14½ per cent. per annum, and interest on the amount so allowed each subscriber, from July 1, 1867, to January 1, 1868, at the rate of 7 per cent. per annum; and the secretary and treasurer be instructed to make statement of, and pay to each subscriber, the amount under this resolution.

*Resolved*, That a dividend of 6 per cent. per annum be, and is hereby, declared for each of the years ending the 1st day of November, 1866 and 1867, payable in stock of the Union Pacific Railroad Company, at 30 per cent. of its par value, to the registered stockholders of this day.

In conformity with the above resolutions, interest and dividend statements have been prepared, and will be paid on application to the undersigned.

Respectfully,

BENJAMIN F. HAM,
*Assistant Secretary and Treasurer.*

*Report of the treasurer to the stockholders of the Credit Mobilier of America.*

The treasurer begs leave to report that since the last annual meeting at Philadelphia the company have been rigorously prosecuting the construction of the Union Pacific Railroad under contract, and have expended up to the present time, as shown by the books of the company, about $5,500,000; have completed some seventy miles of road, with some one hundred and fifty miles ready for superstructure, and have a large lot of material and supplies on hand. On 3d March last, by resolution of the board of directors, with the approval of the stockholders, the capital stock of the company was increased to $2,500,000, the whole amount being subscribed for and nearly all paid in.

The total receipts up to this date were—

| | |
|---|---|
| Capital stock | $2,365,915 00 |
| Union Pacific Railroad Company | 2,633,162 31 |
| Sundry accounts | 125,361 46 |
| Total | 5,124,438 77 |

The total disbursements:

| | | |
|---|---|---|
| Construction contract | $3,433,574 03 | |
| Stock Union Pacific Railroad Company | 515,410 00 | |
| Scrip Union Pacific Railroad Company | 848,172 50 | |
| Interest account | 185,754 33 | |
| Sundry accounts | 141,527 91 | |
| | | 5,124,438 77 |

[illegible]

[illegible] subscribers [illegible]

[illegible], one thousand [illegible]

[illegible], two hundred [illegible]

[illegible], two hundred [illegible]

[illegible], five hundred [illegible]

[illegible], one hundred [illegible]

[illegible], five hundred shares.

[illegible], two hundred shares.

---

WASHINGTON, *January* [illegible]

[illegible] sworn and examined.

[illegible] reside?—Answer. Cambridge, Ma[illegible]

[illegible] connected with the Union Paci[illegible] [illegible] since when, and in what capacity?—[illegible] [illegible] March, 1871.

Q. Mr. Durant paid you the $30,000?—A. He paid me a much larger amount than that.

Q. Did you have an accounting with Mr. Durant with regard to the large amount that came into your hands?—A. Now, I will answer that question just as it transpired, and you must bear with me, as my answer may, perhaps, save other questions. When the basis was determined upon which these matters in dispute should be settled, it was reduced to a memorandum, the parties having this memorandum. A man claimed a hundred thousand dollars' worth of stock, or he would claim that equivalent, or some other equivalent, in land, that would possibly be settled for ten per cent. of the amount or fifteen per cent.—the best terms that could be effected to avoid litigation—all the claims having at least some color to maintain them, and sometimes very well-defined obligations. These memoranda—whatever the amount was, ten, fifteen, or twenty per cent., for in no instance did it go above twenty per cent. to any one person—were grouped together, and Mr. Hallett on the one part would approve them, for before I concluded the settlement I had consulted sufficiently close with him and Mr. Durant to know what would be acceptable to them. These were reduced to a general memorandum, upon which the bonds were to be delivered. If the party relinquished what he had in the way of a claim, he received this memorandum that he would get so many bonds, and when these were all brought together, they were paid, and the memoranda taken in. There was no other mode of settlement.

Q. Taken in by whom?—A. By Durant and Hallett.

Q. What time did you get these bonds?—A. The latter part of June, 1864. Now, as to my own employment; the records of Congress will advise you that when the Kansas Pacific Railroad, as it is now called, was sold to Hallett and Frémont, it gave rise to a series of controversies between parties who were interested in the road previous to that, who had certain claims upon it. During the fall of that year Mr. Hallett and Mr. Frémont differed and separated, which eventuated in Mr. Durant coming into the Union Pacific, eastern division. That is the road commencing at Kansas City and going back to Denver, and forming a junction with the main line at Cheyenne. That gave rise to contest and litigation between Hallett and Frémont. After it had been well ascertained that the road could not be built under the act of 1862, and when, in 1864, they were seeking here to get further strength in their financial condition by the friendly legislation of Congress, among other embarrassments, there sprung up a contest between Hallett and Frémont, each well sustained by counsel, the quarrel having commenced in New York, and found its way here and in the committee-room. Mr. Dudley Field and certain other gentlemen were brought here as counsel, and what was known as the eleventh section of the act of 1864 was got into the bill as reported—mark you, as reported, for it never became a law. When that eleventh section was put in, it provided that the Leavenworth, Pawnee and Western Railroad, commonly known as the Union Pacific, eastern division, should have neither land nor bounty until the controversies, represented as they were by two boards of directors, Frémont president of one and Perry the other, should be settled or determined by a court of competent jurisdiction; and in that shape, with that clause in the bill, it was reported from the committee on the Pacific Railroad. I was engaged more especially to handle what was called the Hallett and Durant side of the controversy, and it was our design to get the bill free from that clause. It was in connection with that that I took an active part, and for that reason you will understand that the bonds

"NEW YORK, *December* 12, 1872.

"Whereas it appears by the report of the finance committee, submitted this day, that the company will require about four millions of dollars for the payment of coupons and obligations maturing on or before April 1, 1873; and whereas the income bonds of the company, amounting to ten millions of dollars, mature in 1874: It is therefore

"*Resolved*, That a mortgage upon the land, land-grants, road-bed, appurtenances and property of the company be made to the Union Trust Company, of New York, as trustees, to secure the payment of the bonds of this company for sixteen millions of dollars currency, or three millions two hundred thousand pounds in British sterling, in sixteen thousand bonds, numbered 1 to 16,000 inclusive, for the sum of $1,000 United States currency, or £200 British sterling each, the principal of which is payable on the 1st day of March, 1903, in gold, unless sooner redeemed under the sinking-fund clause hereinafter contained, at the office of the company, with interest at the rate of 8 per cent. per annum currency, or 7 per cent. per annum British sterling, at the option of the holder, interest payable on the 1st day of March and the 1st day of September in each year, said bonds to be called "a sinking-fund mortgage bond."

*Resolved*, That a sinking fund of one per cent. per annum on the amount of coupon bonds actually issued and outstanding under the mortgage be created for the purchase, at par, and extinguishment of said coupon bonds issued under this mortgage, to be redeemed by annual drawings by lot, by the trustees for the time being, or some one of them, or by some person duly authorized by them, in the month of February in each year, beginning in the month of February, 1874, at the office of the Union Trust Company, or their satisfactory successors, in New York, in the presence of one of the officers of the company and of a notary public, notice of said drawing to be announced thirty days prior to said drawing, both in New York and London, and notice of the numbers so drawn to be posted, by the trustees for the time being, at the office of the Union Trust Company, in New York, and at the office of Morton, Rose & Co., in London, or their satisfactory successors, and also to be advertised, by the Union Trust Company and Morton, Rose & Co., in one or more newspapers in each of the cities of New York and London. On the 30th day of August following the drawing, the bonds so drawn shall be paid, by the trustees for the time being, to such of the holders thereof as may have, in writing, notified the trustees on or before that day of their election, to have their bonds so redeemed or paid; that is to say, at the rate of $1,000 in United States currency in New York, or £200 in British sterling money in London, for each bond, on delivery of the bonds with the unmatured coupons. And in case any of the holders of the bonds so drawn shall fail to notify the trustees, in writing, of their election to have their said bonds thus paid and redeemed, as aforesaid, then and forever thereafter such bonds shall cease to be entitled to be purchased and redeemed by means of said sinking fund shall be proportionately reduced.

"*Resolved*, That ten millions of dollars, or two million pounds sterling, of the above bonds, known as the ten per cent. income bonds of this company, and for no other purpose whatever.

"*Resolved*, That the aforesaid coupon bonds may, at the option of the holder, be converted into registered bonds of the company, bearing interest at the rate of 8 per cent. per annum in currency, said registered bonds not being entitled to share in the sinking fund or annual dr under said sinking fund.

*Hoxie Contract.*

| | |
|---|---|
| Charged | $12,550,278 94 |
| Charged August 4, 1869: bills payable | 2,000,000 00 |
| | 14,550,278 94 |
| Credited | 14,813,899 07 |
| Balance Cr | 263,620 13 |

Q. Did your book-keeper make up the statement in reference to the Hoxie contract?—A. He did.

Q. State what has been the whole cost of this railroad to the Union Pacific Company, as shown by the books of the company?—A. ... 7.12.

Q. Does this paper which you have put in evidence show, as far as ... from the books, the cost of the construction of the whole ... various contracts?—A. It does.

... amount of first mortgage bonds were issued by the Union ... Company?—A. $27,237,000.

... other class of bonds been issued by the Union Pacific ...?—A. Yes.

...?—A. Land-grant bonds; $10,400,000.

... these land-grant bonds have been disposed of?—A.

... they issued?—A. I will furnish the committee with a ... the amount issued and the amount redeemed.

... what amount of money the Union Pacific Rail- ... first-mortgage bonds?—A. Yes, sir.

...—A. I will cause to be made up a statement ... which the Union Pacific Railroad Company ... gage bonds.

... the Union Pacific Railroad Company derive ... bonds?—A. I will furnish a statement of ... realized about their par.

... bonds, whether sold to a large or small ... in the books of the company?—A. Yes.

... Company any account with the ... books?—A. It has.

... Company, according to the ...?—A. It does not.

... [after referring to the books.] The ... $92,466.37, as a balance due th... The last entry in that account i...

... Credit Mobilier with the Union ... August, 1869?—A. [After ... to have been ... on that date, $705,89... the Union Pacific Ra... —A.

Q. ... the c... that ... not.

To what amount?—A. We have $220,000 of the Utah Southern oad bonds.

State the transaction.—A. We furnished the iron and rolling- for that road, agreeing to take in return for it the bonds and of the company. I think we also have, as collateral, Utah Cen- ailroad bonds and Colorado Railroad bonds.

To what amounts?—A. I would not undertake to fix the precise nts.

Will not your books show?—A. Not the books that I have here.

Has there been an actual outlay of money by the Union Pacific oad Company on account of those roads?—A. There has been on nt of the Utah Central, because the Union Pacific Railroad ot succeed in placing those loans immediately after it fur- d the money and materials.

How much money of the Union Pacific Railroad Company is now ted in that way?—A. It is but justice for me to say that it was oney of the company. The money was furnished by the di- rs of the company.

Which of the directors did it?—A. Nearly all the present board rectors have done it.

Who are the present board?—A. Horace F. Clark, Augustus ll, James H. Banker, Oliver Ames, John Duff, Elisha Atkins, s Ames, L. P. Morton, R. E. Robbins, James Brooks, G. M. Dodge, ey Dillon, C. S. Bushnell, George M. Pullman, F. G. Dexter.

Were those Utah Central bonds furnished during the progress of work, or after its completion?—A. I think after the completion of road.

. If the directors or officers of the Union Pacific Railroad furnished money with which to take those bonds, what had the Union Pacific road Company to do with them?—A. They furnished the money to company, and the company furnished it to the Utah Central Rail- d.

Q. So that the company now owes this money to its own directors?— Yes, sir.

Q. And the company owns these bonds as its collateral security for e redemption of the money?—A. Yes, sir.

Q. Why was that thing done?—A. For this reason: It was deemed ry much to the advantage of the Union Pacific Railroad to have a ilroad constructed from Ogden to Salt Lake, and thence further south, , by that means, they would have direct communication with Salt ake City by rail, and with the mineral region below in the Utah val- ey. All the freight and passenger traffic between the Utah valley and he East must go over every mile of the Union Pacific Railroad Com- pany.

Q. Is there on the books of the company what is known as an item f special legal expenses?—A. There are on the books of the com- pany legal expenses; there is a legal-expense account.

Q. Do you know an item of $125,000 for special le[illegible]nses?—A. I know an item of about that amount, but not exac[illegible]unt.

Q. Do you know what it was fo[illegible] I think [illegible] which I have here shows it.

Q. Refer to it.—A. At the dir[illegible]g held [illegible] 1871, the following resolut[illegible] [illegible] committee of three be appointe[illegible] the pr[illegible] ttle, and pay the special legal e[illegible] compe[illegible] date." This was at *the regular* [illegible] doubted that Congress would pass the bill were buying the stock while I was selling. They all of them got badly taken in. They were lame ducks.

Q. From whom did you acquire the original lot that you had?—A. I had purchased it. I was carrying it on speculation.

Q. From whom did you purchase it?—A. From one of the brokers in New York; Mr. Clews, I think. There were three or four men buying stock for me. I do not recollect from whom I bought it.

Q. Did you get any of it from any of those managers of the Union Pacific Railroad Company?—A. No, sir.

Q. Did you get any of it that you did not get by purchase?—A. There may have been some carried for me. For instance, I furnish information to a gentleman, and he says, "If you give me this information, I will carry for you one, two, three, four, or five hundred shares and pay you whatever it appreciates from the time I buy." I may have had, and probably had some stock of that kind at that time.

Q. Who was carrying stock for you at that time?—A. Several brokers.

Q. Give us their names.—A. I am not going to disclose to the committee my private transactions in New York. They do not relate to Congress.

The CHAIRMAN. That is for the committee to determine.

The WITNESS. There is nothing in them relating to Congress in the slightest degree. I do not choose to have my private transactions and operations in New York inquired into, and therefore I decline to answer the question. I will say to the committee that nobody connected with Congress in any shape or form had anything to do with my transactions, directly or indirectly.

The CHAIRMAN. But we have something to do with others besides members of Congress. I will vary the form of the question a little and ask you to state whether any person who was connected with the management of the Union Pacific Railroad Company was carrying any of the stock for you?—A. No, I think not.

Q. Was Mr. Durant carrying any for you?—A. No.

Q. Was Mr. Bushnell?—A. No.

Q. Was Sidney Dillon?—A. No.

Q. Oakes Ames?—A. No, sir.

Q. Was Oliver Ames?—A. No, sir. Not one of these men had I any transaction with.

By Mr. HOAR:

Q. What is there in the transaction of carrying stock for you a short time by a New York broker that makes you unwilling to disclose his name?—A. I do not think it is part of the business of this committee to inquire into my private transactions.

Q. But what is there in the fact that you should be unwilling to disclose?—A. I would rather people should not know what I am doing. That is all. I cannot discover why I should disclose my private business when it has no relation to anything that this committee is authorized to inquire into.

Mr. HOAR. I want to know what there is in it that makes you unwilling to disclose it.

The WITNESS. I do not want to disclose any of my private matters. I prefer not to let other people know what my private business is.

Mr. HOAR. You have stated what your business is, and the question is as to the names of the brokers.

The WITNESS. I have stated that Mr. Clews has done a great deal of business for me.

I wish to state that I know nothing whatever of the use that was made of this money, or whether it was used to employ counsel ordinary or otherwise.

By the CHAIRMAN:

Q. Have you at any time had any interest in the Credit Mobilier of America?—A. Yes, sir; I had, as I stated to the committee of which Mr. Poland is chairman.

Q. What interest did you have in that corporation?—A. An interest of ten shares of the stock.

Q. Were you at any time an officer of that corporation?—A. No, sir.

Q. When did you acquire that ten shares?—A. My recollection is, as I stated in my testimony before the other committee, that it was in or about the month of May, 1868.

Q. Did you acquire that as an original subscription, or did you purchase it?—A. I purchased it.

Q. From whom?—A. From Mr. Oakes Ames.

Q. How long did you hold that stock?—A. I held it until some time in the winter of 1868–'69. I cannot recollect the date that I parted with it.

Q. You got it in 1868, and disposed of it in the winter of 1868–'69?—A. Yes.

Q. Have you held any interest in it since the winter of 1868–'69?—A. No, sir.

Q. In your capacity of Government director have you had occasion to examine the books of the Union Pacific Railroad Company, with a view to ascertaining the cost of construction under the different contracts that had been made for the construction of this road?—A. No, sir. When I became a Government director the construction of the road was completed; the construction had been all made; and, in fact, the tracks between the Union and the Central Pacific roads had been joined. I had given some attention, however, to the cost of the road in order to make up my judgment as to whether or not too much money had been expended in it.

Q. Have you examined the books of the Union Pacific Railroad Company with reference to that question?—A. Not critically. I have at times examined them and got statements.

Q. Have you ever given any attention to the question as to what the Hoxie contract cost the Union Pacific Railroad Company?—A. No, sir; I have not, except in this: I had occasion once to investigate a question connected with the Hoxie contract, and in that I came to the conclusion that the road had cost too much under that contract.

Q. Do you recollect the amount that you considered as the excess paid under the Hoxie contract?—A. I do not recollect.

Q. About what time was it that you made this investigation in reference to the Hoxie contract?—A. It was in the winter of 1870 or the spring of 1871.

Q. Do you recollect seeing an item of $2,000,000 which had been added to the cost of construction under the Hoxie contract?—A. I do not recollect.

Q. Have you any recollection now of your attention having bee[illegible] tracted to an item of that kind?—A. No, sir; I have not.

Q. Has your attention ever been called to the fact that, on 4t[illegible] 1869, the Union Pacific Railroad Company gave a note for $[illegible] and then charged that up to the Hoxie contract?—A. I do [illegible]

I wish to state that I know nothing whatever of the use that was made of this money, or whether it was used to employ counsel ordinary or otherwise.

By the CHAIRMAN:

Q. Have you at any time had any interest in the Credit Mobilier of America ?—A. Yes, sir; I had, as I stated to the committee of which Mr. Poland is chairman.

Q. What interest did you have in that corporation ?—A. An interest of ten shares of the stock.

Q. Were you at any time an officer of that corporation ?—A. No, sir.

Q. When did you acquire that ten shares ?—A. My recollection is, as I stated in my testimony before the other committee, that it was in or about the month of May, 1868.

Q. Did you acquire that as an original subscription, or did you purchase it ?—A. I purchased it.

Q. From whom ?—A. From Mr. Oakes Ames.

Q. How long did you hold that stock ?—A. I held it until some time in the winter of 1868–'69. I cannot recollect the date that I parted with it.

Q. You got it in 1868, and disposed of it in the winter of 1868–'69 ?—A. Yes.

Q. Have you held any interest in it since the winter of 1868–'69 ?—A. No, sir.

Q. In your capacity of Government director have you had occasion to examine the books of the Union Pacific Railroad Company, with a view to ascertaining the cost of construction under the different contracts that had been made for the construction of this road ?—A. No, sir. When I became a Government director the construction of the road was completed; the construction had been all made; and, in fact, the tracks between the Union and the Central Pacific roads had been joined. I had given some attention, however, to the cost of the road in order to make up my judgment as to whether or not too much money had been expended in it.

Q. Have you examined the books of the Union Pacific Railroad Company with reference to that question ?—A. Not critically. I have at times examined them and got statements.

Q. Have you ever given any attention to the question as to what the Hoxie contract cost the Union Pacific Railroad Company ?—A. No, sir; I have not, except in this: I had occasion once to investigate a question connected with the Hoxie contract, and in that I came to the conclusion that the road had cost too much under that contract.

Q. Do you recollect the amount that you considered as the excess paid under the Hoxie contract ?—A. I do not recollect.

Q. About what time was it that you made this investigation in reference to the Hoxie contract ?—A. It was in the winter of 1870 or the spring of 1871.

Q. Do you recollect seeing an item of $2,000,000 which had been added to the cost of construction under the Hoxie contract ?—A. I do not recollect.

Q. Have you any recollection now of your attention having been attracted to an item of that kind ?—A. No, sir; I have not.

Q. Has your attention ever been called to the fact that, on 4th August, 1869, the Union Pacific Railroad Company gave a note for $2,000,000, and then charged that up to the *Hoxie contract* ?—A. I do not think I ecutive committee, but I live 1,200 miles away from the place of meeting, and of course I cannot run back and forth every day to attend these meetings, and therefore the information which I, with the other Government directors, would get would be mainly at the quarterly meeting of the board of directors, when we would take up and read what the executive committee had done.

Q. Did you ever protest against the action of this executive committee as a Government director?—A. I have frequently done so.

Q. Did you do it formally, so as to enter your protest on the minutes of the board?—A. I do not know whether such a thing can be found on the minutes; but it has been done in discussions of the board. I have objected very emphatically in the meetings of the board of directors to having the action of the board of directors undone by the executive committee.

Q. You protested earnestly against this coal contract?—A. Yes, sir; I have been at war upon that for two or three years.

Q. Were you a member of Congress in 1864?—A. Yes, sir.

Q. What, if anything, do you know in reference to a change of route from Sioux City, in Iowa, to Omaha?—A. When the bill of 1862 was reported from the Pacific Railroad Committee it provided for an Iowa branch, the main trunk commencing not farther west than the one hundredth meridian. I was not satisfied with the shape of the bill. I was at that time practically the only Representative in the House from the State of Iowa, my colleague, General Vanderveer, being in the Army. I secured an amendment to the bill, under which the Omaha line was built. In connection with one or two members from Minnesota, I waited on the Committee on the Pacific Railroad, and induced them to put in also the Sioux City branch. The provision of the act of 1862, as nearly as I can recollect it, was that the Union Pacific Railroad Company should construct that Sioux City branch whenever a road was constructed through Iowa from the East terminating at Sioux City When the bill of 1864 was under consideration our State had six members of the House. Mr. Hubbard, from the then sixth district, resided at Sioux City. He was very anxious to have a railway connection as early as possible from his section of the State. In the mean time the Dubuque and Sioux City Railroad Company had become involved in financial difficulties, and were not pushing their road. Mr. Hubbard concluded that he could get the connection sooner by having the road constructed by an independent company, and without waiting for the action of the Dubuque and Sioux City Company, and therefore, in his amendment he provided for releasing the Union Pacific Railroad Company from constructing the Sioux City branch, and for authorizing some company to be organized in Iowa or elsewhere to construct that branch.

Q. The change was made in the act of 1864 authorizing this Sioux City branch to be constructed by another company, which was then organized, or which might thereafter be organized, I believe?—A. Yes; I think that was in the provision.

Q. Was there a company at that time organized, under whose charter that Sioux City branch was afterward constructed?—A. The company which constructed the Sioux City branch was not organized at the date of the passage of the act of 1864.

Q. When was it organized?—A. It was organized some time during at year.

'. Has that company built the road?—A. Yes, sir.

of that company. I have been connected with it as a stockholder. I was a stockholder in 1865.

Q. Are you still a stockholder?—A. I am.

Q. And have you been all the time since you first became a stockholder?—A. Yes.

Q. Have you been in any way engaged in the management of the Credit Mobilier?—A. No, sir.

Q. You had no relation to it other than as a stockholder?—A. No other.

Q. Do you know of a contract having been made with Oakes Ames for the construction of any part of the Union Pacific Railroad?—A. I do.

Q. Was there any work done by Oakes Ames under that contract prior to its assignment?—A. I cannot say. The contract was assigned within a month or two months after it was made. My impression is that there was no work done under the contract until after the assignment to the trustees.

Q. At the time that contract was made what was your business relations to Oakes Ames?—A. We are partners in business and have always been.

Q. At the time that contract was made, and also at the time it was assigned, what were your official relations to the Union Pacific Railroad Company?—A. I was president of the company.

Q. Are you the Oliver Ames who executed that contract on behalf of the Union Pacific Railroad Company?—A. I am.

Q. When that contract was assigned it was assigned to a board of trustees?—A. It was.

Q. Were you one of that board of trustees?—A. I was.

Q. Are you still a trustee under that contract?—A. I am.

Q. And have been continuously ever since the assignment?—A. Yes, sir.

Q. Was there any other contract made by the Union Pacific Railroad Company for the construction of road of that company after the Oakes Ames contract?—A. There was the Davis contract.

Q. That had reference to that portion of the road lying west of the Oakes Ames contract?—A. Yes.

Q. Was that Davis contract assigned to the same board of trustees?—A. It was.

Q. At the time the Davis contract was made what official connection did you have with the Union Pacific Railroad Company?—A. I was president of the company.

Q. Were you president of the company also at the time of the assignment of the Davis contract?—A. I was.

Q. This assignment was made to the same board of trustees as the assignment of the Oakes Ames contract was made to?—A. The same board of trustees. I think Mr. Alley was not on the board of trustees at that time, although he was on the original board.

Q. Did this board of trustees, pursuant to the Oakes Ames contract, proceed to the construction of the road embraced in that contract?—A. It did.

Q. And did construct it as it has been constructed?—A. Yes.

Q. Did the board of trustees, pursuant to the Davis contract, proceed to the construction of the road embraced in that contract?—A. It did.

Q. And constructed it as it has been constructed under that contract?—A. Yes.

Q. Have you the books and papers of that board of trustees showing

Q. Was it to Congressmen that he intended to dispose of it?—A. He mentioned others besides Congressmen.

Q. Did he mention Congressmen as persons to whom he intended to dispose of some of this stock?—A. Yes, he mentioned Congressmen as persons to sell the stock to.

Q. Do you recollect now any Congressman that he mentioned except Mr. Colfax?—A. I think he mentioned Mr. Boutwell.

Q. Anybody else?—A. I think he mentioned Mr. Wilson too; he boarded at that time with Mr. Wilson.

Q. Who else?—A. I do not recollect very distinctly about the names of the parties.

Q. Do you remember any other name that he mentioned?—A. I do not. I know very well the names that are now before the public in that connection, but I do not remember any other now that he mentioned at that time.

Q. Why was he going to let members of Congress have it? Was it because of the pecuniary aid that he expected to derive, or because he desired to get the influence of members of Congress by disposing of the stock to them?—A. Well, I suppose it was because he desired to get a good class of people in it. We did not expect that any legislation would be necessary; we had got all the legislation we wanted.

Q. Well, was it money that he was after in making that disposition of the stock or was it influence?—A. It was money that he was after.

Q. Money especially?—A. Yes, sir.

Q. And the influence of these parties was not what he was seeking?—A. No, sir; but then we all desire always to be associated with good men.

Q. Did Mr. Oakes Ames inform you that he had disposed of that stock and to whom he had disposed of it; and, if so, when did he give you that information?—A. Well, sir, I cannot answer that question. I have a general idea that he did dispose of it to such parties as hold it or as have held it along, and whose connection with it has now come out. I have that general idea about it; but it is possible that that may have been impressed upon my mind recently.

Q. Did you ever know anything personally as to what disposition he had made of the stock?—A. No, sir; I never did.

Q. What was the date of the assignment of that stock to your brother, Mr. Oakes Ames?—A. It was in 1867, I think.

Q. Was it not in January, 1868?—A. (Referring to book.) It was in January, 1868; two hundred and twenty shares and thirty shares.

Q. Congress was then in session?—A. It was.

Q. Was your brother at the place where the assignment was made at that time?—A. I do not know. I was not an officer in this company, and of course I don't know anything about that.

Q. The arrangement for transferring that stock to your brother was made prior to the date of that assignment?—A. Yes, sir.

Q. Was it made before he went on to Congress?—A. I think it was made in the April previous to January, 1868; I think so, from what I now know of the matter.

Q. Was the amount of the stock that was to be transferred to him in trust to dispose of, definitely agreed upon at that time?—A. I think it was.

Q. What was the amount?—A. I do not recollect the amount. I recollect my brother saying that he could dispose of so much stock; that had promised so much stock; he made a little statement of so much cerned. I saw no wrong in it to anybody, unless they wronged themselves.

By Mr. SWANN:

Q. Is it the custom now in the State of Massachusetts—for I consider that State badly dealt with by the opinion you have just given—whenever the Secretary of the Treasury orders an inspection of the national banks, which he does from time to time, for these banks, whenever they are short of the required amount of specie or currency, to go to another bank which may be hard by, and borrow the amount of specie or currency which is necessary to make up their balance-sheet?—A. No, sir; I do not mean to say any such thing, or intimate any such thing.

Q. Would you not consider that a fraud upon the public?—A. Why, certainly I should.

By the CHAIRMAN:

Q. By the assignment of the Oakes Ames contract, it was stipulated that the parties who were to participate in the dividends or avails of that contract should sign an irrevocable proxy, authorizing these trustees to vote six-tenths of the stock they held in the Union Pacific Railroad Company?—A. Yes, sir; until the completion of the contract.

Q. Was this six-tenths more than a majority of the stock of the Union Pacific Railroad Company?—A. I do not know how that was.

Q. Was it intended to be a majority of the entire stock of the Union Pacific Railroad Company?—A. I do not know that it was intended to be. It was regarded as sufficient to control the company, with the additional stock that was owned by themselves individually.

Q. And they were to give an irrevocable proxy to vote not only the stock they owned then, but the stock they acquired by virtue of the Credit Mobilier?—A. The object was to keep control, and I think every consideration of prudence required it, over the road until the contract was finished.

Q. Were these proxies given?—A. Yes, sir; I believe so.

Q. Do you know who held these proxies?—A. I think Mr. Oliver Ames, chairman of the board of trustees, held them.

Q. Do you remember that, at a meeting held in New York on the 27th January, 1868, you offered a resolution that was adopted, authorizing Oliver Ames to vote these proxies?—A. I presume so, if the record says so. I have no recollection of it.

Q. Do you know for what length of time Mr. Ames held these proxies and used them?—A. I do not think they were ever used but once.

Q. Were they not used twice?—A. In 1868 they were used for the first time. I think Mr. Ames testifies they were used in 1867, but he must be mistaken, for at the annual meeting in 1867 they had not been completed; and I do not think they were used in 1869, but they may have been.

Q. But it is a fact that the proxies were given in pursuance of the Ames contract?—A. Yes, sir.

Q. Then the parties who held the Union Pacific stock and the Credit Mobilier stock were the same parties substantially?—A. They were when the Oakes Ames contract was made. They shifted very much afterward. I should say in 1868 they were not.

Q. But that is substantially the fact, is it not?—A. It was before the Oakes Ames contract was signed.

Q. Was it not after the Oakes Ames contract?—A. It was not at the time of the election.

Q. Still, the effect of the execution of these proxies was to place the control of the Union Pacific Railroad entirely into the hands of these seven trustees to whom the Oakes Ames contract was assigned?—A. That was the object of it.

Q. Well, that was the effect of it, was it not?—A. It must have been if they held a majority of the stock.

Q. So, if it turned out to be a fact that they held a majority of the stock, then, by virtue of this irrevocable proxy, the entire management and control of the Union Pacific Railroad was taken away from that corporation and put into the hands of these seven trustees?—A. No, sir; not all.

Q. Well, they held the voting power?—A. They held the voting power provided they held a majority of the stock.

Q. My question is predicated upon the supposition that they did have a majority of the stock.—A. The record will show how that is.

Q. Did not the Hoxie contract extend from Omaha to the hundredth meridian, and was not two hundred and forty-seven miles of the road built under that contract?—A. Yes, sir.

Q. And after that contract had been completed and the road built up to the hundredth meridian, there was a proposition to extend the contract over fifty-eight miles more of the road?—A. I do not know that the proposition was made. I know that it was expected they should have the contract for extending the road.

Q. But there was a proposition to extend the contract over that fifty-eight miles of the road?—A. I have an impression that there was; I am not positive.

Q. At the time this effort was made to extend the contract over this fifty-eight miles of road, had not that fifty-eight miles been already constructed and accepted by the Government?—A. That I do not know. It was built really by the Credit Mobilier, and with their funds.

Q. I am not talking about who built it; had it not already been accepted by the Government?—A. That I cannot say.

Q. Do you remember Dr. Durant filing a protest against the extension of the Hoxie contract over this fifty-eight miles of road?—A. I do not.

Q. Were you not connected with the road at that time?—A. I do not remember; I do not know what the date was.

Q. Do you know what that fifty-eight miles of road had cost?—A. I do not know.

Q. When the Oakes Ames contract was made, had there not been one hundred and thirty-eight miles of road constructed and accepted by the Government west of the hundredth meridian?—A. I do not know. I should say very nearly that.

Q. Had there not been a very considerable amount of track laid that had not been accepted by the Government—between eighty and one hundred miles?—A. That I cannot say anything about.

Q. My object in putting these questions is to give you an [illegible] to explain to the committee why it was the company gave a [illegible] for the construction of one hundred and thirty-eight miles of [illegible] had already been constructed and accepted by the [illegible] do not know that I can tell exactly, but my recollection [illegible] it was expected, as I have said before, that the [illegible] go on and complete the road, and it had purchased [illegible] materials, and paid for them, and the capital of the [illegible] been almost entirely absorbed by the Union Pacific [illegible] in the building of the road, &c. There was quite [illegible] the settlement of this *claim, the* Credit Mobilier [illegible]

Q. Have you examined the New York books with reference to th matter?—A. No, sir.

Q. Have you ever examined the New York books, with reference t either of these contracts?—A. No, sir. The New York books did n come to the Boston office till about a month before I left.

Q. Does that trial-balance sheet, show the state of the accounts b tween the Union Pacific Railroad Company and the Credit Mobilier?—A. Yes, sir.

Q. What does it show on the subject?—A. It shows that the Cred Mobilier was debtor to the Union Pacific Railroad Compan $816,285.01.

Q. What was that date?—A. May 1, 1871.

Q. At the time you made that up, had this $2,000,000 been entere up on the books of the company?—A. I should say that it had bee but I cannot tell without referring to the books.

Q. That sheet does not show it.—A. No, sir; this is merely balance from the books.

Q. Do you know of any sales of bonds or subscription of stock tha was made during the time you were connected with the Union Pacifi Company, and with those trustees?—A. I have such knowledge as could obtain by being in the office.

Q. What do you know of the sale of bonds?—A. I do know of th sale of bonds being made by the Union Pacific Company.

Q. What bonds were they?—A. All the bonds that the compan owned.

Q. What class of bonds were they?—A. Some income and some lan grants, and some bridge bonds.

Q. Do you recollect what amount in all was sold?—A. Betwee $4,000,000 and $5,000,000.

Q. To whom were they sold?—A. They were sold to Mr. C. A. Bushnell, as agent.

Q. As agent for whom?—A. I do not know that fact.

Q. Do you know at what rate they were sold?—A. Yes, sir.

Q. What was it?—A. The income bonds were sold at 50 per cent., the land-grant bonds were sold at 70 per cent., and the bridge bonds were sold at 85 per cent.

Q. What bridge bonds do you refer to?—A. The Missouri River bridge which crosses at Omaha.

Q. About what time was that sale of bonds?—A. About January 1, 1871.

Q. State whether there was any sale or subscription of stock at or about that time?—A. The trustees sold some stock.

Q. To whom did they sell that stock?—A. To the same parties.

Q. What parties do you mean?—A. The parties whom Mr. Bushnell represented.

Q. How did the trustees get that stock; from what source did they get it?—A. I do not know that I can answer.

Q. Was there a subscription of stock about that time on the books of the Union Pacific Railroad Company, and, if so, who made it?—A. Yes, sir; I think there was a subscription.

Q. Who subscribed?—A. Mr. John A. Rice, assistant treasurer of the trustees.

Q. What was the amount of stock that was sold by those trustees at the time you indicated?—A. From 20,000 to 30,000 shares.

Q. Was there any money paid to the Union Pacific Railroad Comp on account of that subscription, any money paid into the treasury that company?—A. There was an open account which John A. Rice, assistant treasurer of the trustees, had on the books, and there was a credit to his account.

Q. Do you mean to say a credit to the amount of the subscription?—A. I cannot say without referring to the books. The stock subscription books will not show it, but the general ledger kept in Boston will show it.

Q. Look at this subscription by Rice on the stock subscription book and state whether that is the subscription you refer to?—A. (After looking at the book.) I should say it was one of those subscriptions.

Q. What is the amount of it?—A. Thirty thousand shares.

Q. What is the date of it?—A. July 29, 1870.

Q. How was that subscription of 30,000 shares paid for?—A. I cannot say unless it went into John A. Rice's account on the ledger. There was no formal transaction.

Q. Was there any money paid?—A. There was a nominal check passed, I believe, but no money.

Q. It was a paper transaction exclusively, was it?—A. Yes, sir.

Q. Describe that paper transaction. Tell the committee exactly how this thing was done?—A. The vouchers are in the office, and they had better speak for themselves.

Q. I simply want you to state how it was done—whether it was done by passing checks or by paying in money?—A. Just by passing a check on the Bank of Commerce, and a receipt was made out for the check.

Q. Was there any money in the Bank of Commerce to the credit of the Union Pacific Railroad Company corresponding with any such sum as that?—A. No, sir.

Q. The Union Pacific Railroad Company got no such sum of money as that in actual money?—A. No, sir. It would depend somewhat on how much these thirty thousand shares represented. If it was a dollar a share, it might have been paid, but if the shares were at par it could not be.

Q. Was there any money paid on account of that sale of bonds?—A. Yes, sir; the day the transaction was consummated there was a check for $500,000 passed in payment for 1,000 income bonds. The rest of the bonds which were sold were out, pledged as collateral; and as the loans matured on which these bonds were pledged, the bonds were turned over, the party taking it paying for the bonds.

Q. Do you know what the purpose of that transaction was; this sale of bonds and subscription of stock?—A. It was to enable the company to pay their floating debt.

Q. Was there any change in the ownership of the road, or in the control of the road, at or about that time?—A. This transaction was some time in January; there was a change of direction in March.

Q. Do you recollect who came to be the directors in March?—A Colonel Scott came in as president, and two or three new directors can in.

Q. Do you recollect who they were?—A. I cannot recall their nam There were one or two from the Pennsylvania road. They calle Scott interest, or the Pennsylvania interest.

Q. State just how the Union Pacific Railroad Comp that thirty thousand shares of stock which were issu A. If Mr. Rice subscribed for that stock and paid fo longed to the trustees. The trustees made the thousand shares of stock to the same party.

two million and some odd thousand dollars. That remained some until it was necessary to use this note, and then the note was giv that account.

Q. Please find that on the records of the Union Pacific Railroad pany?—A. (Reading.) "March 28, 1867. Mr. Sherman reported a lows: The committee to whom the account with the Credit Mobilie referred report that the vouchers for an item which at our last r was not furnished have been now produced, and we have exan them and found them satisfactory. We therefore report that there due on the Hoxie contract on the 31st of January, 1867, $1,994,7C which, when paid, should be a full and complete settlement of that tract for the construction and equipment of the road from that poi the 100th meridian. On motion, the report was accepted and the acc ordered to be paid." Now this balance had been made up by me, o half of the Union Pacific Railroad Company, and by Mr. Crane, who represented the Credit Mobilier, before I had anything to do witl Credit Mobilier. We had come to this as the balance due on that tract, and it was adjusted then by the directors of the Union P Railroad Company and acknowledged as a credit.

Q. That, then, makes the cost of the road from Omaha to the 1 meridian $14,290,835.90?—A. No, sir; I did not so state. I stated there might be charged in that $14,290,835.90 some money that wa pended on the road beyond the 100th meridian.

Q. Give us the amount that had been paid out on the Hoxie con prior to that time?—A. The amount paid on the Hoxie contract the 30th of March, 1867, was $13,381,342.33.

Q. Is this amount that was allowed by the board in that sum: That was the balance.

Q. Was this $1,994,769.96 embraced in that $13,381,342.33?—A. but there was another item. There was an item of $406,926.09 fo terest. That should be deducted from the $13,381,342.33.

Q. That leaves $12,974,416.24; that amount had been paid up to time?—A. Up to the 1st of January, 1867.

Q. You observe that that resolution which you read a moment only embraces the road between the one hundredth meridian Omaha?—A. Yes, sir.

Q. They found out in some way how much was due on the Hoxie tract at that time, did they not?—A. What they did was to take money that they had paid Hoxie, and which was already charge him in the books, and credited him with this item, and that lef balance so much.

Q. State now how much it cost the company to build the road u the Hoxie contract from Omaha to the one hundredth meridian?- Twelve million nine hundred and seventy-four thousand four hun and sixteen dollars and twenty-four cents. That was the amount justed between the two companies.

Q. Have you the exact length of the road from Omaha to the hundredth meridian?—A. Yes, sir; 246.72 miles.

Q. That at $50,000 a mile amounts to what?—A. Twelve mil three hundred and thirty-six thousand dollars.

Q. That makes the Hoxie contract cost the company $638,416.24 m than the contract price?—A. No, sir; it does not; because it was st lated in the contract that the company should pay certain extras, they did pay them.

Q. That is the way you account for the difference between the tract price and what was paid?—A. Yes, sir. The contract provi that if any of the bridges cost over $85,000, they would pay the difference; and there was one bridge that cost over $167,000. They paid also for burnetizing the ties and timbers; that was $20,000; and there was also extra cost of transportation. The company abandoned part of the line, too, and Mr. Hoxie was paid for work on that abandoned line $70,000.

Q. Do you mean that that was paid to Mr. Hoxie, or to the Credit Mobilier?—A. It was paid under the Hoxie contract.

Q. It was paid to the Credit Mobilier?—A. No, sir; it was paid under the Hoxie contract.

Q. Who had that contract?—A. That was before I had anything to do with it; it was before I came.

Q. As a matter of fact, the Hoxie contract was transferred to the Credit Mobilier?—A. Mr. Crane can tell you that positively.

Q. It was paid on that contract at all events?—A. Yes, sir.

Q. What did it cost the company to build the next fifty-eight miles of road?—A. That I cannot tell you.

Q. Before passing from that, tell us what it cost the Credit Mobilier to build the road up to the one hundredth meridian?—A. Seven million eight hundred and six thousand one hundred and eighty-three dollars and thirty-three cents.

Q. Did the Credit Mobilier make other profits beyond the one hundredth meridian?—A. Yes, sir; under the Oakes Ames contract they were entitled to the profits on fifty-eight miles.

Q. How much were they?—A. There was $1,104,000, I think, paid on account of that. It never was adjusted.

Q. That is what it was estimated at?—A. No, sir; that is simply a sum that the trustees wanted to pay the Credit Mobilier, and they paid that much. I do not know just how that was made up, but I know that was the sum that was paid.

Q. Can you tell how much money was paid out on that fifty-eight miles by the Union Pacific Railroad Company, or by the Credit Mobilier, in its construction?—A. No, sir; I cannot.

Q. Is there any mode by which that can be ascertained from the books?—A. I don't think there is.

Q. So that there is no way of ascertaining the cost of construction of the fifty-eight miles?—A. No; I don't think there is.

Q. All that you can tell about it is that in an adjustment between the Credit Mobilier and these trustees there was $1,104,000 awarded to the Credit Mobilier as profits upon that fifty-eight miles of road.—A. It was not an adjustment.

Q. What was it?—A. It was simply so much paid on account.

Q. Does the Credit Mobilier claim that there is anything more coming to that corporation on that account?—A. It has been claimed that it should be adjusted when the final settlement came.

Q. How is it proposed to be adjusted?—A. I don't know.

Q. Is there any mode by which it can be adjusted except by a guess?—A. I don't know that there is; possibly there may be; I don't know how to get that fifty-eight miles by itself; I might have done it four or five years ago, but it would be a pretty difficult matter now.

Q. On the 15th of November, 1867, or before that time, had you up an account of the profits made by the Credit Mobilier ur date?—A. I don't know that I had.

Q. Look at that letter-book and say if you wrote that let state to what you referred in that letter, if you did write i able to make remunerative returns hereafter to the persons who so p in that $30,000,000?

The WITNESS. With friendly relations with the Government, I th it would unquestionably make returns.

Mr. HOAR. How remunerative?

The WITNESS. You are dealing in unknown quantities and the fu of railroads is all uncertainty.

Mr. HOAR. Do you not think that, with the resources which the qu tion I have put supposes, there would be such a vast development business between the Atlantic and Pacific as would make the retu on such an investment highly remunerative?

The WITNESS. I think it would make remunerative returns. I not understand exactly what you mean by highly remunerative. A r road to make returns that are remunerative must be able to maint itself in a good condition, and pay 8 per cent. to its stockholders. Th I should call a remunerative road. I should want more than that fo highly remunerative road. I should not look for that in a great ma years from the Union Pacific Railroad.

Q. Not with those resources?—A. No, sir; I think there is no tra that requires any very large expenditure, except for the maintenance the track. It is a tolerably well completed road. Your thirty milli dollars I do not think would add much to the earnings. It wo give solvency and strength. But I think that if it had thirty milli in its treasury now the bulk of it should be at once appropriated to t payment of its debts. That is what I should advise.

Q. It would remove the embarrassments occasioned by its present i debtedness and probable insolvency?—A. I think there is no man co nected with railroads that does not know that there is danger in deb

Mr. HOAR. The object of my question, I will explain to you, is to certain, if I can, what would have been likely to be its history suppo ing that the capital stock had been actually and in good faith paid in cash instead of its having been subscribed under contracts by which reality, as some witnesses say, the company got, instead of 100 per ce in cash, 30 per cent. in road-building for every share of its capital sto The object of my question is to learn of the present president of t road what, in his judgment, would have been likely to have been its co dition and the value of the property to the men who built it if that h not been done.

The WITNESS. It is entirely conjectural. I am hopeful as to the futu growth and settlement of the country. I think that, in respect of this ro it is as well established as many other roads, and that there will be a lar increase of its traffic. I do not think that it needs any very immense e penditure on it, any very serious outlay. If the company had that mon and did not owe a debt, I think it might divide a good deal of it amo the stockholders.

Q. Suppose the road was obliged to rely upon its own credit and business, without the individual aid of anybody, could it, in your jud ment, meet its obligations in the course of business for the next twel months?—A. I think [illegible]

Q. Suppose the [illegible], as you understand it, were to [illegible] the acts of 186[illegible], would t [illegible] obligations [illegible] of b [illegible] directo [illegible] ma [illegible] e

million [illegible] actually [illegible]
[illegible] effected on such conditions [illegible]
[illegible] think that economy was possible. I think that [illegible]
[illegible] was more extravagant than anything I e[illegible]
[illegible] when the work was done—the outside expen[illegible]
[illegible] possible [illegible]
[illegible] expenditures do you mean —[illegible] In the first pla[illegible]
[illegible] own. They had to build a road from [illegible]
[illegible] enormous [illegible]
[illegible] the Missouri River from [illegible]

[illegible] speaking of the wastefulness and extra[illegible]
[illegible] do you mean to imply an expen[illegible]
[illegible] do you mean to imply an [illegible]
[illegible] existing condition of things [illegible]

[illegible]

treasury to pay for the entire construction of the six hundred and sixty-seven miles as Mr. Ames built it, they could have found responsible contractors in the market who would have built it cheaper than he did?—A. I do not. You could have found irresponsible men who would have taken the contract, but would not have performed it.

Q. Could they not have found responsible contractors who would have built it any cheaper?—A. I think not. And let me say that I think it was the wildest contract that I ever knew to be made by a civilized man. That is my judgment and my belief.

Adjourned.

---

WASHINGTON, D. C., *January* 30, 1873.

Continuation of the testimony of HORACE F. CLARK.

By the CHAIRMAN:

Question. In your testimony yesterday you based some of your opinions and calculations on the question of coal for the use of the road; do you know when coal was first discovered on the line of the road?—Answer. I remarked yesterday that I had no connection with the road at that time, and all that I knew of it was its general history. I believe that there had been reports that Indians had brought in from the plains specimens of coal. There were rumors about coal, and men who were very hopeful in regard to the enterprise supposed that they would find coal. I suppose it was because of their conclusions from the geological formation; but as to an amount of coal accessible for railroad purposes, my impression was that it was as late as 1864 or 1865 that the fact was ascertained. I remember to have heard before 1867 that the Union Pacific Railroad Company was paying $19 a cord for what in New England would be called brush.

Q. You spoke of that matter of coal in connection with the contract made with Oakes Ames?—A. My attention was not called to the question of the contract with Oakes Ames. No mention was made of it in my examination. My impression was that the road would be good for nothing unless available coal for railroad purposes had been discovered. I made no reference to the Oakes Ames contract, nor do I know the date when it was made.

Q. Did you not say that, when you heard of the Oakes Ames contract, you thought it was the wildest that was ever made?—A. I did say that.

Q. And did you not at that time also make this observation in reference to the discovery of coal?—A. I meant my observation as to the coal question to apply to the running of the road, when built, not to the Oakes Ames contract. The reason why I thought the Oakes Ames contract a wild adventure was because it was building the road [illegible] the fuel question unsettled.

[illegible] derstand that the fuel question was unsettled when [illegible] was made, in August, 1867, and when it was [illegible] A. I should think that at that time the [illegible] coal deposits accessible would be found. [illegible] report of Dr. Durant, which was made [illegible] to the surveys made up to the close [illegible] 1865?—A. Never, except as part of [illegible] not recollect that particular re-about what did you consider it as worth in cash?—A. I did not consider that it had any market value at all.

Q. Do you mean that it had no intrinsic value, or do you simply mean that it was not quoted in the market?—A. I mean that you could not borrow money upon it or you could not sell it.

Q. It was not considered worth anything?—A. You could not sell any considerable portion of it, except to people who would take a risk as they would at a faro-bank.

Q. So it was estimated really in the letting of this work as of no appreciable value?—A. At that time we looked forward to the time when the road would be completed, and the country settled, and when the stock would be of value.

By the CHAIRMAN:

Q. Was there no price of the stock talked about at that time?—A. I do not recollect; I had nothing to do with the details of the contract.

By Mr. HOAR:

Q. Were you an experienced person in railroad construction or management at the time you went into that direction?—A. Yes, sir.

Q. What had been your experience; was it in railroad finances, or in railroad building, or in both?—A. In both. I have been in the Hannibal and Saint Joseph Railroad Company, and got $600,000 in stock, which I offered to take 10 per cent. for rather than take the stock, so that the value of railroad stock before the road is built is not much.

Q. You, as a director and a party in interest in the Union Pacific Railroad Company, knew something, of course, of the nature of the route over which the road was to be built at the time the Oakes Ames contract was made?—A. Not fully; only as to a portion of it. I had been through the Platte Valley, and knew something of the character of the country there.

Q. You stated, in answer to Mr. Shellabarger, that the price of the work was put up on account of receiving part of the pay in stock.—A. I did not say that the price was put up, but the price was larger on that account, of course.

Q. The price of the road was greater, because the payment to the contractor was made in stock, and not in cash?—A. Yes.

Q. In your judgment, was the amount of the two classes of bonds received from the company by the contractor enough to pay a fair price for the construction of the road, without counting in the stock at all?—A. No; I think it was not.

Q. How much do you think it would fall short?—A. I cannot tell you exactly; there was no market at that time for the first-mortgage bonds. The market had to be created, and the bonds popularized.

Mr. HOAR. I am not speaking merely about their price in the market, but about their actual value.

WITNESS. The market price is the actual value. I estimate what a bond or stock is worth by what it will bring in the New York stock market.

Mr. HOAR. I am asking about what you regard as the actual, int[illegible] value of the two classes of bonds.

WITNESS. At that time I would not have considered th[illegible] gage bonds worth more than 50 cents on the dollar, and th[illegible] bonds 80 cents. I think that the Government bonds wer[illegible] know that I bought a good many for 90, and had them [illegible]

Q. Leaving out now any question of legality or ill[illegible]

Q. When did you first become a stockholder?—A. That I can't t[ell] you.

Q. When did you first become a stockholder in the Credit Mobili[er?] —A. April 20, 1865.

Q. Were you in Washington at the time that the legislation of 18[..] was pending?—A. No, sir.

Q. Do you know anything in regard to this "suspense account" whi[ch] has been spoken of?—A. I do not.

Q. Was that matter ever before the board of directors of the Unio[n] Pacific Railroad Company when you were present?—A. No, sir.

Q. Have you ever heard that matter discussed in the board?—A. [I] have not, sir.

Q. Have you ever heard the individual members of the board discussing that?—A. I have not; I had nothing to do with it.

Q. Were you in Washington at the time the legislation of 1871 was pending?—A. No, sir.

Q. Were you at the meeting of the board when this item of $126,000 was under consideration?—A. I don't know whether I ever heard it spoken of at all, the $126,000 that you speak of. I live in New York, and the board is in Boston; and I don't know whether I was there at the time that you have been speaking about to-day or not; I might have been there, but if I was, as I knew nothing about the transactions going on around Washington or anywhere else, I knew nothing about this, and never heard anything about it.

Q. Do you know anything about it now?—A. I do not.

Q. Do you know of any moneys having been paid by any person or persons connected with the Union Pacific Railroad Company to any member of Congress or officer of the Government?—A. I do not.

Q. Directly or indirectly?—A. No, sir.

Q. Have you any information of such moneys having been paid?—A. Nothing only what I have heard in this room.

Q. Were you present at the time that the proposition was made to extend the Hoxie contract over a portion of the road that had been already constructed?—A. I might have been, but I do not bear it in mind.

Q. Do you remember the fact that that thing was attempted to be done?—A. Well, I can remember that there was some talk about it; but that is all I can remember.

Q. Do you know the object of extending that contract over fifty-eight miles of road that had been already constructed?—A. Which contract?

Q. The Hoxie contract. Do you remember a proposition that was made by J. M. S. Williams?—A. I remember that there was a proposition made.

Q. Do you remember that, at the time it was made, he had agreed in writing that he would assign that contract to the Credit Mobilier?—A. How long a contract?

Q. Fifty-eight miles or more.—A. I think that is the fact, but I cannot swear positively about it.

Q. What was the purpose of extending that Hoxie contract over that piece of road that had been already constructed?—A. I am not able to say.

Q. Was it for any other purpose than to put profits into the treasury of the Credit Mobilier?—A. I can't tell you; I do not recollect that part of it.

Q. You do not recollect what did take place?—A. I do not.

Q. At the time the Oakes Ames contract was let there was a lar[ge] [illegible] making attempts of [illegible]

[illegible] having been done?— [illegible] That matter was about a long time [illegible] the bragging of a man [illegible]

[illegible]?—A. No, sir. I would [illegible] the Union Pacific Railroad Company [illegible], and I never came to Washington to get a bill [illegible] I believe, and I hope [illegible] again on account of the Credit Mobilier.

—

WASHINGTON, D.C., *February* 1, 1873.

[illegible] recalled and examined.

By the CHAIRMAN:

Q. [illegible] state again, so that it may be conveniently known by the committee in this connection, what your relation was to those trustees.—A. [illegible] I was their secretary and assistant treasurer up to the time that they moved their office to Boston. I was appointed permanent secretary of the trustees, and I consider myself their secretary yet, but [illegible] they took their matters to Boston I have had nothing to do with them [illegible].

Q. Was the principal part of their business done with before they went to Boston?—A. It was.

Q. The contracts that they were interested in had been substantially performed and the moneys received from the Union Pacific Railroad Company?—A. Yes, sir.

Q. Have you looked through the books that have been brought here to see whether all the books of the trustees are here?—A. I do not [illegible]

Q. What seems to be wanting?—A. All the transactions that have [illegible] to Boston—the books that [illegible]

Q. [illegible] the Oakes Ames [illegible] the trustees up to the time [illegible] from New York?—A. No, sir.

[illegible]

pany in that particular form?—A. That was simply a little error, probably in writing the resolution. I called my part special expenses, and I called General Dodge's part, although he is not a lawyer, legal expenses.

Q. What were General Dodge's relations at that time to the Union Pacific Railroad Company?—A. He was pretty sore toward it at that time.

Q. Was he chief engineer at that time?—A. No, sir; I think he was a director at that time.

Q. General Dodge was one of the committee to settle that account, was he not?—A. It is my impression that he was.

Q. Do you know his handwriting?—A. I think so.

Q. (Showing the witness the report given in the testimony of E. H. Rollins.) Is this report, which was made to the board at that time, in his handwriting?—A. I think it is.

Q. Who received the $19,000 check?—A. I received all the checks myself.

Q. Who were present at the time you received them?—A. I do not recollect anybody being present in the cashier's room except Mr. Williams, Mr. Spence, and the clerks. Mr. Spence was one of the clerks. Mr. Williams, I think, handed them to Spence, and Spence handed them to me. I handed General Dodge his and Colonel Scott his; I do not recollect distinctly about Mr. Rollins, but probably I handed him his. The balance I handed over to Mr. Williams.

Q. You received $82,500. What was the object of dividing that up into three different drafts?—A. These land-grant bonds were hypothecated in different places and for various amounts. To get this money to pay we had to get bonds, and in order to get the bonds we had to pay money. So far as I recollect, these particular drafts were payable in the different places where the bonds were.

Q. Do you recollect whether the bonds were in the banks on which the drafts were drawn, or did the bonds accompany the drafts?—A. The bonds were scattered around in the banks in New York and in Boston. I took the drafts and took up the bonds, and let the bonds go forward with the drafts. They went on frequently with the drafts, and sometimes without them.

Q. In this particular instance did the bonds go forward with the drafts?—A. That I do not recollect; that thing did occur frequently.

Q. Look at this memorandum [as presented in the testimony of B. W. Spence] and state in whose handwriting these figures and words are.—A. I cannot tell that.

Q. Are they in yours?—A. I would not say that they are not, but still I cannot say that they are.

Q. What is your best impression about it?—A. I do not think they are mine.

By Mr. HOAR:

Q. I understand you to say that previous to this transaction you had engaged to purchase from the Union Pacific Railroad Company certain securities?—A. Yes.

Q. Did you at that time make your contract in writing?—A. I think it was in writing.

Q. With whom did you make any such agreement or co think with the executive committee of the Union I Company.

Q. What members of it; what persons?—A. Oliv Mr. Dillon. What others I cannot recollect now.

Q. Was there anything in the bargain except an agreement on your rt to purchase these securities at the prices you have named ?—A. nd to pay for them as the loans matured; that is all.

Q. To what persons connected with the Government or the Union cific Railroad Company did you, at the time of this approval of the 26,000, explain or make known how it was made up ?—A. I declare I not recollect anybody.

Q. You said that you made a statement; to whom did you make it ?— To the board of directors.

Q. Did you explain to the board of directors how this $126,000 for al expenses was made up ?—A. Not in detail.

Q. Did you explain the nature of the transaction as you have ex- ined it here ?—A. Not as fully.

Q. Did you to anybody ?—A. No, sir.

Q. By what authority did you take from the funds of the Union Pacific ilroad Company this sum of $126,000 and charge it to special legal penses ?—A. By the same authority that I gave them half a million llars more than the market price for the securities when I bought em.

Q. I want to know who authorized the payment to you of this sum of 26,000 so far as you know ?—A. The board of directors appointed committee.

Q. Were you one of that committee ?—A. No, sir.

Q. To what members of that committee did you explain that trans- ion ?—A. To the president of the company.

Q. Mr. Oliver Ames ?—A. No, sir; Mr. Scott.

Q. To any other person ?—A. Yes; to General Dodge.

Q. Was General Dodge a director in the company at that time ?—A. s; and he was on this committee. I do not think that the other mbers of the committee took any action at all or attended.

Q. You had no previous promise from the company by which you were be paid this $126,000 ?—A. I think it was a matter of conversation h several of the directors that I might need help, and that if I did hould have it.

Q. You took this $126,000, and the only persons to whom you ex- ined why you did it were Mr. Scott, who you say had $19,000 of it, l Mr. Dodge, who you say had $24,500 of it ?—A. Yes.

Q. And you three were the three gentlemen who knew about it, and charged it to special legal expenses ?—A. Special and legal was the lerstanding.

Q. Mr. Dodge's report seems to agree with the charge upon the books. says: "The special committee of the board to which was referred mattter of auditing *special legal expenses.*"—A. The record may not re been properly copied, but I know it was *special and legal.*

Q. The phrase, "special legal expenses," is found first in the resolu- n of the directors appointing the committee, then in the report of neral Dodge, and then on the ledger. It seems to be a permanent or ?—A. Yes; but the first mistake was in writing the resolution, l the others all followed naturally.

Q. Why mix up an item for legal expenses of $24,500, or whatever it s, with this item of yours for getting help from the company on ac- nt of the contract which you had previously made ?—A. This was an anized meeting of the board, [illegible] there would [illegible] another for ee months. This was the [illegible], if at all, [illegible] should have ef.

Q. But it was not for your [illegible] paid his

pany in that particular form?—A. That was simply a little error, probably in writing the resolution. I called my part special expenses, and called General Dodge's part, although he is not a lawyer, legal expenses.

Q. What were General Dodge's relations at that time to the Union Pacific Railroad Company?—A. He was pretty sore toward it at that time.

Q. Was he chief engineer at that time?—A. No, sir; I think he was a director at that time.

Q. General Dodge was one of the committee to settle that account, was he not?—A. It is my impression that he was.

Q. Do you know his handwriting?—A. I think so.

Q. (Showing the witness the report given in the testimony of E. H. Rollins.) Is this report, which was made to the board at that time, in his handwriting?—A. I think it is.

Q. Who received the $19,000 check?—A. I received all the checks myself.

Q. Who were present at the time you received them?—A. I do not recollect anybody being present in the cashier's room except Mr. Williams, Mr. Spence, and the clerks. Mr. Spence was one of the clerks. Mr. Williams, I think, handed them to Spence, and Spence handed them to me. I handed General Dodge his and Colonel Scott his; I do not recollect distinctly about Mr. Rollins, but probably I handed him his. The balance I handed over to Mr. Williams.

Q. You received $82,500. What was the object of dividing that up into three different drafts?—A. These land-grant bonds were hypothecated in different places and for various amounts. To get this money to pay we had to get bonds, and in order to get the bonds we had to pay money. So far as I recollect, these particular drafts were payable in the different places where the bonds were.

Q. Do you recollect whether the bonds were in the banks on which the drafts were drawn, or did the bonds accompany the drafts?—A. The bonds were scattered around in the banks in New York and in Boston. I took the drafts and took up the bonds, and let the bonds go forward with the drafts. They went on frequently with the drafts, and sometimes without them.

Q. In this particular instance did the bonds go forward with the drafts?—A. That I do not recollect; that thing did occur frequently.

Q. Look at this memorandum [as presented in the testimony of B. W. Spence] and state in whose handwriting these figures and words are.—A. I cannot tell that.

Q. Are they in yours?—A. I would not say that they are not, but still I cannot say that they are.

Q. What is your best impression about it?—A. I do not think they are mine.

By Mr. HOAR:

Q. I understand you to say that previous to this transaction you had engaged to purchase from the Union Pacific Railroad Company certain securities?—A. Yes.

Q. Did you at that time make your contract in writing?—A. I hardly think it was in writing.

Q. With whom did you make any such agreement or contract?—A. I think with the executive committee of the Union Pacific Railroad Company.

Q. What members of it; what persons?—A. Oliver Ames, Mr. Dil- Mr. Dillon. What others I cannot recollect now.

ıs there anything in the bargain except an agreement on your purchase these securities at the prices you have named?—A. ›ay for them as the loans matured; that is all.

what persons connected with the Government or the Union ailroad Company did you, at the time of this approval of the , explain or make known how it was made up?—A. I declare I ›collect anybody.

u said that you made a statement; to whom did you make it?— ıe board of directors.

l you explain to the board of directors how this $126,000 for ›enses was made up?—A. Not in detail.

l you explain the nature of the transaction as you have ex- t here?—A. Not as fully.

l you to anybody?—A. No, sir.

what authority did you take from the funds of the Union Pacific Company this sum of $126,000 and charge it to special legal ?—A. By the same authority that I gave them half a million nore than the market price for the securities when I bought

ant to know who authorized the payment to you of this sum of so far as you know?—A. The board of directors appointed nittee.

›re you one of that committee?—A. No, sir.

what members of that committee did you explain that trans- -A. To the president of the company.

. Oliver Ames?—A. No, sir; Mr. Scott.

any other person?—A. Yes; to General Dodge.

ıs General Dodge a director in the company at that time?—A. d he was on this committee. I do not think that the other of the committee took any action at all or attended.

u had no previous promise from the company by which you were d this $126,000?—A. I think it was a matter of conversation eral of the directors that I might need help, and that if I did have it.

u took this $126,000, and the only persons to whom you ex- why you did it were Mr. Scott, who you say had $19,000 of it, Dodge, who you say had $24,500 of it?—A. Yes.

d you three were the three gentlemen who knew about it, and ged it to special legal expenses?—A. Special and legal was the nding.

. Dodge's report seems to agree with the charge upon the books. : "The special committee of the board to which was referred tter of auditing *special legal expenses*."—A. The record may not n properly copied, but I know it was *special and legal*.

e phrase, "special legal expenses," is found first in the resolu- he directors appointing the committee, then in the report of Dodge, and then on the ledger. It seems to be a permanent A. Yes; but the first mistake was in writing the resolution. others all followed naturally.

ıy mix up an item for legal expenses of $24,500, or whatever it h this item of yours for getting help from the com- ... the contract which you had previously made?—A d meeting of the board, and there would not nths. This was the proper time, if at all, that

t it was not for your relief that General Dod

ment?—A. If he was president during that time, as I think he was, he did.

Q. He knew of the fact of your getting the consent of all the stockholders of the Union Pacific Railroad Company that the Credit Mobilier, composed as it was of the men who were running the Union Pacific Railroad Company, should have the contract to build the road, thus making, in fact, a bargain with themselves. He knew of that if he was president and did his full duty?—A. I think he knew of everything that was going on, and he didn't see anything wrong.

Q. You think he knew of everything that has been brought out here, and approved of it?—A. Yes, sir.

Q. You think he earned his $8,000 a year in approving of those things?—A. Yes, sir.

By Mr. HOAR:

Q. Did General Dix remain president after he went abroad?—A. Yes, sir.

Q. How long?—A. Until the next election; I do not remember the exact date.

Q. Do you know whether this Credit Mobilier contract and the transactions connected with it were during General Dix's presidency or during the presidency of Mr. Oliver Ames?—A. The only contract the Union Pacific Railroad Company ever had with the Credit Mobilier of America was under the direction of and executed by General Dix.

Q. Under that contract there was a dividend of 12 per cent. to the Credit Mobilier?—A. Yes, sir.

Q. And there was only one dividend?—A. Yes, sir.

Q. The subsequent contract under which these large dividends were made, was that executed under General Dix or Oliver Ames?—A. The execution of it, if I remember, was by Mr. Ames, in the fall of the year, but it should not be lost sight of, in this investigation, that the real fact was that this Oakes Ames contract was a matter of understanding and agreement early in the spring of 1867, but it did not take shape and execution until the fall, and during the intermediate time this one hundred miles of road was built.

Q. Now it is important to know whether General Dix, so far as your knowledge extends, was president of the road at the time that understanding was had?—A. It is my memory that he was. I don't know whether the committee have found out, but I have never seen it published, the fact that we never made one single dollar to my satisfaction in building the Union Pacific Railroad east of Cheyenne or west of Carbuncle. We made our whole money in an incredibly short time in building the road from Cheyenne, one hundred and fifty miles west, but not a dollar can be shown that we made west of that one hundred and fifty miles, and I do not believe we made one dollar east of Cheyenne. It was a fortunate circumstance that the Rocky Mountains were not what we anticipated they would be, and but for that lucky strike we would have lost money. We got $96,000 a mile for building that piece of road, and it didn't cost us so much as that for which we got $61,000 a mile, and the nation ought to know that had the Rocky Mountains been what we thought they would be, we would never have got out of that contract with one single dollar in our pockets.

By Mr. SHELLABARGER:

Q. I will ask you a question here, whether you agree with Mr. [illegible] that the nature and character of [illegible] through the Rocky Mountains was known in 1863?—A. He [illegible] known it; nobody else had that the paper on which the name is written has been rubbed; there is also a marked difference in the ink used.

Q. Was there a check issued for $2,500 the same day, March 9, 1871?

A. There seems to have been a check issued March 9, 1871, for $2,500.

Q. Have you that check?—A. I have.

Q. Will you produce it?—A. I have it.

Q. Read it.—A. "National Bank of Commerce, Boston, March 9, 1871; pay to the order of B. W. Spence twenty-five hundred dollars; (Signed) "John M. S. Williams, treasurer, No. 2374." In the upper left-hand corner, $2,500 in figures; indorsed, "Pay Hon. E. H. Rollins, or order. B. W. Spence." Indorsed, "E. H. Rollins," pay J. Carr, esq., cashier, or order, for collection for First National Bank, Concord, New Hampshire, J. J. Crippen, acting cashier. Following that, "C. H. Draper, acting cashier."

Q. On what account was that check given?—A. That was given for money which was borrowed for Mr. Bushnell.

Q. Where?—A. At Washington.

Q. From whom?—A. From Mr. Ordway.

Q. Does that form any part of the $126,000?—A. All the checks and drafts covering the $126,000 presented to me for indorsement were, agreeably to the report of the special committee, indorsed by me as secretary. This check was not indorsed by me as secretary, and is evidently not included in that amount.

Q. Was this check of $2,500 paid out of the earnings of the Union Pacific Railroad Company?—A. It would appear from the books that the check was exchanged for a draft of Mr. Bushnell's on M. Morgan Sons, of New York, for the same amount.

Q. How is the balance of the $126,000 paid, as appears by the books of the company?—A. The balance, in addition to the two checks, one for $24,500 and one for $19,000, was paid by three drafts on M. Morgan Sons, of New York, as follows: One for $43,841.09; one for $18,632.46; one for $20,626.45.

Q. Have those drafts come back to the Union Pacific Railroad Company?—A. They have not.

Q. Mr. Spence, in his testimony, has spoken of an item of $3,500 paid to you in 1870. Are there any entries on the books in regard to that sum, or any other sum, charged to legal expenses? If so, state what the entry is, and on what account the money was paid.—A. An entry seems to have been made on the cash-book as follows: "Legal expenses debtor to cash for amount advanced E. H. R., June 1, by order of Oliver Ames, and now charged as above, by direction of E. H. R. $3,500."

Q. In whose handwriting is that entry made?—A. In the handwriting of Mr. Spence.

Q. Was that entry made there by your directions, as entered in the book?—A. From the entry, I presume that I gave the order, though I do not remember distinctly.

Q. On what account was that money used?—A. It was advanced at the time, at the request of Mr. Ames, and allowed me for services rendered the company. I never received a dollar [illegible] Pacific Railroad Company in my life for [illegible] have I had a dollar that I did not earn by ha[illegible] no money expended for political purposes [illegible] became treasurer of the company, and I thi[illegible] will not be under the present administra[illegible] [illegible] represented in its b[illegible]

ton; for the next three years, at five dollars per ton; for the fo
thereafter, at four dollars per ton; and for the six years remai
the rate of three dollars per ton, delivered upon the cars at th
of said party of the second part, and which shall not be less t
per cent. added to the cost of the same to the said party of the
part. This contract to be and remain in full force for the full
fifteen years from the date hereof.

That the said railroad company agrees to facilitate the operat
said party of the second part, in prospecting and otherwise, by
of such information as it may possess, and by furnishing free pa
its road to the agents of the party of the second part not excee
in number.

The said railroad company further agrees to put in switches
necessary side-tracks at such points as may be mutually agre
for the accommodation of the business of the said party of th
part.

That the said party of the second part agrees to make all
exertions to increase the demand and consumption of coal
parties along the line of said railroad, and to open and op
at such points where coal may be discovered as may be dev
railroad company, and to spend within the first five ye
date of this agreement, in the purchase and development
mining-lands and in improvements for the opening, succe
nomical working of the same, not less than the sum of tw
dollars; also to furnish for the use of said railroad
merchantable coal, and to pay all expenses for improvem
coal into cars. Any improvements desired by said railr
regard to the coal to be used by it shall be at the cost
company.

In consideration of their exertions to increase th
and the large sum to be expended in improvements, i
that the party of the second part shall have the righ
the said railroad and its branches, for the next fift
date of this agreement, coal for general consumptio
that will be charged to others; but the said party
shall be entitled, (in consideration of services re
vided,) to a drawback of twenty-five per cent. on
transportation of coal.

The said railroad company agrees to furnish t
part such cars as they may require in the ope
and to transport them as promptly as possil
remain in force for fifteen years.

The coal-lands owned by said party of the fir
for the full term of fifteen years to the s
part, or their assigns, for the purpose of work
to them profitable; said party of the second
nine years, a royalty of twenty-five cents p
taken from their lands, excepting always
courses or passage-ways, for which coal no
ment for the same being due and payable
last six years of this lease shall be fre
the railway is reduced to three dollars
twenty-five cents per ton, or more
be as during the first nine yea

*List of stockholders Union Pacific Railroad Company, &c.*—Continued.

| | | | | | |
|---|---|---|---|---|---|
| 36 | Baker, Ezra H., jr | 297 | 146 | Davis, Wm. H | [illegible] |
| 36 | Bangs, A. W | 12 | 146 | Daniels, David H | [illegible] |
| 37 | Bates, B. E., Treas. of trustees. | 1,141 | 153 | Drexel, Morgan & Co | [illegible] |
| | | | 154 | De Von, F. R | [illegible] |
| 38 | Barstow, Rogers L | 15 | 156 | Dillon, Sidney | [illegible] |
| 40 | Black, Geo. W | 2 | 158 | Dillon, Mrs. Hannah | [illegible] |
| 42 | Bates & Brown | 2,410 | 163 | Dodge, G. M | [illegible] |
| 43 | Bradford & Stanton | 100 | 163 | Dorrance, E. B | 5 |
| 44 | Bangs, Coffin & Co | 54 | 164 | Dotger, A. J | [illegible] |
| 47 | Bend, Wm. B | 1,300 | 165 | Duff, John | [illegible] |
| 49 | Briggs, H. O | 60 | 166 | Duff, John R | [illegible] |
| 49 | Briggs, Edwin | 80 | 170 | Durant, Thos. C | 4 |
| 49 | Bliss, E. C. W | 6 | 174 | Durant, T. F | [illegible] |
| 51 | Briggs, Lloyd | 100 | 174 | Duncan, Sherman & Co., in trust. | [illegible] |
| 51 | Bristol, Wm. B | 100 | | | |
| 52 | Baldwin, L. D | 100 | 185 | Eno, John C | [illegible] |
| 59 | Boissevain Bros | 440 | 186 | Elex & Brockerman | [illegible] |
| 62 | Brooks, James | 490 | 187 | Everett, J. Mason | [illegible] |
| 63 | Brewster, Sweet & Co | 200 | 187 | Evans, T. B | [illegible] |
| 64 | Boocock, Sam'l | 300 | 187 | Evans, Wharton & Co | [illegible] |
| 65 | Boyd, Vincent & Co | 100 | 187 | Ewell, Wood & Co | [illegible] |
| 67 | Bloodgood, John & Co | 1,400 | 192 | Fahr, Charles | [illegible] |
| 70 | Bullard, Lewis H | 10 | 195 | Francis, Chas. B | [illegible] |
| 70 | Bush, Richard D., trustee | 21 | 197 | Fanshan & Milliken | [illegible] |
| 71 | Butler, Peter | 7 | 199 | Fessenden, Sewell H | [illegible] |
| 72 | Bushnell, C. S | 711 | 199 | Fessenden, Geo. L | [illegible] |
| 76 | Berlin & Hymans | 200 | 202 | Fish, James, jr | [illegible] |
| 78 | Banker, James H | 100 | 204 | Fellows, James W | [illegible] |
| 81 | Baldwin & Kimball | 750 | 206 | Fellows & Co | [illegible] |
| 82 | Benedict, Flower & Co | 100 | 214 | Ford, N. & Sons | [illegible] |
| 82 | Baylis, A. B. & Co | 700 | 214 | Foster, Pierpont B | [illegible] |
| 85 | Brown, Geo. & Sam'l & Co. | 50 | 224 | Gray, H. W | [illegible] |
| 86 | Becker & Fuld | 220 | 227 | Gray, H. W. & Co | [illegible] |
| 88 | Bunge, Wm. & Co | 150 | 229 | Gardner, Chas. P | [illegible] |
| 91 | Chapman, Oliver S | 1,497 | 236 | Gilbert, Horatio J | [illegible] |
| 92 | Chavlick, Oliver | 309 | 237 | Gilmore, Wm | [illegible] |
| 94 | Carpenter & Richards | 100 | 237 | Gilmore, Alson | [illegible] |
| 95 | Chase & Higginson | 1,720 | 237 | Gilmore, Edwin | [illegible] |
| 95 | Clark, Wm. Adolphus | 15 | 237 | Gilmore, Mary E | [illegible] |
| 97 | Chase, Geo. H | 20 | 238 | Gilmore, E. W | [illegible] |
| 98 | Champ, James | 600 | 239 | Glidden, Wm. T | [illegible] |
| 99 | Carnegie, Andrew | 100 | 240 | Glidden, John A | [illegible] |
| 102 | Capron, R. J. & Co | 7,300 | 244 | Glendenning, Davis & Amory. | [illegible] |
| 102 | Clark, Enoch | 30 | | | |
| 102 | Clark, A. P | 75 | 244 | Grimes, James W | [illegible] |
| 104 | Carter, Timothy J | 100 | 252 | Grinnell, Geo. B. & Co | [illegible] |
| 104 | Clark, James N | 20 | 259 | Gordan, Wm. A | [illegible] |
| 108 | Credit Mobilier of America | 1,890 | 261 | Gourlay, Amanda G | [illegible] |
| 111 | Clark, Horace F | 200 | 262 | Hawley, W. N | [illegible] |
| 112 | Cisco, John J. & Sons | 205 | 262 | Harding, A. C | [illegible] |
| 115 | Colby, Walter | 10 | 263 | Ham Brothers | [illegible] |
| 116 | Coolidge, John T | 980 | 265 | Hazard, Rowland G | [illegible] |
| 117 | Codman, Chas. R | 104 | 268 | Hazard, Roland | [illegible] |
| 117 | Crosby, Geo. L | 13 | 269 | Hazard, Isaac P | [illegible] |
| 120 | Cobb, F. D. & Co | 50 | 270 | Hazard, Mary P | [illegible] |
| 121 | Cooke, Jay & Co | 100 | 270 | Hazard, Elizabeth | [illegible] |
| 122 | Campbell & Richmond | 1,200 | 270 | Hazard, Elizabeth, trustee | [illegible] |
| 123 | Cooper & Graff | 100 | 270 | Hazard, Anna | [illegible] |
| 124 | Crosby, Helen | 4 | 271 | Hazard, Sarah L | [illegible] |
| 124 | Crosby, E. C | 11 | 271 | Haven, Franklin | [illegible] |
| 125 | Crook, Richard L | 200 | 272 | Hawley, T. & Co | [illegible] |
| 130 | Colgate, Edward | 100 | 273 | Hale, Wm. L | [illegible] |
| 130 | Coddington, Jefferson | [illegible] | 274 | Hatch, Rufus | [illegible] |
| 131 | Closon & Hays | [illegible] | 275 | Hatch, Walter T. & Son | [illegible] |
| 132 | Cahen, Joseph | [illegible] | 278 | [illegible], J. H. & Bro | [illegible] |
| 139 | Cutting, R. L., jr. & Co | [illegible] | 279 | [illegible] | [illegible] |
| 142 | Chaplin, Ernest | [illegible] | [illegible] | [illegible] | [illegible] |

*List of stockholders Union Pacific Railroad Company, &c.*—Contin

| | |
|---|---|
| Gilbert, Horatio J | 958 |
| Gilmore, E. W | 1,452 |
| Glidden, John A | 605 |
| Glidden, John M | 735 |
| Glidden, W. T | 4,423 |
| Gray, Francis A | 125 |
| Gray, G. G | 9,030 |
| Gray, H. W | 4,605 |
| Griffing, M. H | 100 |
| Griggs, Salem | 40 |
| Grimes, James W | 2,077 |
| Griswold, J. N. A | 1,009 |
| Guest, W. A | 445 |
| Ham, Benj. F | 3,647 |
| Ham, Benj. F., James M., trustee | 100 |
| Hammond, Henry B | 20 |
| Harding, A. C | 270 |
| Haskins, Ira | 25 |
| Haven & Co | 100 |
| Hawley & Co., T | 225 |
| Hawley, W. N | 90 |
| Hazard, Anna | 143 |
| Hazard, Elizabeth | 160 |
| Hazard, Elizabeth, trustee | 53 |
| Hazard, Isaac P | 2,077 |
| Hazard, Mary P | 101 |
| Hazard, Roland | 2,462 |
| Hazard, R. G | 18,856 |
| Hazard, Sarah L | 100 |
| Hedden, Josiah | 1,000 |
| Hinckley, S. L | 50 |
| Hobart, jr., Aaron | 163 |
| Hodges, F. S | 20 |
| Holliday, Benj | 1,300 |
| Hooper, Samuel, & Co | 6,352 |
| Horner, Anna | 3 |
| Hotchkiss, Henry | 1,212 |
| Hough, B. K | 317 |
| Howland, Gardner G | 300 |
| Hunnewell & Sons, H. H | 1,500 |
| Hurlbert, jr., Henry A | 200 |
| Ingalls, Henry | 100 |
| Ingersoll, J. E | 11 |
| Jencks, B. H | 1,500 |
| Johnson, R. C | 750 |
| Johnston, James B | 3,680 |
| Jones, David | 3,197 |
| Kennedy, G. W | 610 |
| King, John L | 750 |
| Lambard, C. A | 3,051 |
| Lancon, George | 1,700 |
| Lee, N | 20 |
| Lockwood, Le Grand | 2,006 |
| Lord, Thomas | 105 |
| Low, A. A | 735 |
| Macy, Geo. N | 25 |
| Macy, W. H | 2,535 |
| McComb, H. S | 6,092 |
| McCormick, C. H | 8,011 |
| McNeil, R. G. S | 20 |
| Manning, Thomas | 100 |
| Martin, Henry | |
| Maynard & Sons | |
| Means, W. P. M | |
| Mason, W. P | |
| Merrick, G. G | |
| Meyer, E. Reed | |
| Moore, E. C | |
| Morton, Bliss & Co | |
| Nass, William | |
| Neilson, C. H | |
| Nickerson, Frederick | |
| Nickerson, Joseph | |
| Nickerson, Miller W | |
| Nickerson, Thomas | |
| Opdyke, George | |
| Parker, C. H. | |
| Partridge, Warren | |
| Peck, Nathan | |
| Perkins, F. P | |
| Perkins, T. H., guardian | |
| Phelps, James | |
| Pigot, Joseph | |
| Pomeroy, E. H | |
| Pondir, John | |
| Pasmus & Lissignola | |
| Reed, A. A | |
| Reichie, Louis | |
| Ribon, J. J | |
| Rice & Whiting | |
| Richardson, Benj | |
| Richardson, Miss E | |
| Richardson, Joseph | |
| Robbins, Chandler | |
| Robbins, H. A | |
| Robbins, R. E | |
| Rogers, W. C | |
| Sampson, J | |
| Sandford, Henry | |
| Sandford, James H | |
| Scranton, E. S | |
| Scranton, J. H | |
| Sears, Geo. O | |
| Seney, G. J | |
| Shaw, Frank | |
| Skinner & Co., F | |
| Smith, G. P | |
| Smith, O. C | |
| Spencer, A. W | |
| Sprague, C. J | |
| Stetson, Thomas M | |
| Stevens, W. B | |
| Stevens, W. B., trustee | |
| Stevens, jr., W. B | |
| Stevens, Amory & Co | |
| Stone, Daniel | |
| Sturgis, James | |
| Sweetser, Isaac | |
| Ten Harve & Van Essen | |
| Thatcher, Isaac | |
| Thomas, T. G | |
| Torrey, Lydia | |
| Tracy, John F | |
| Trowbridge, E. H | |
| Trowbridge, Henry | |
| Truesdell, L. E | |
| Turner, Seth | |
| Thos | |

| | | | |
|---|---|---|---|
| 1869 | | | |
| Jan. | 6 | To … bought of John Duff | 75,000 00 |
| | 6 | To … on $…, bought by Page, R. & Co., this day, at … per cent | 1,900 00 |
| | [illegible] | To … on $…,000 at … per cent | [illegible] 25 |
| | [illegible] | To $10,000 bought by Page, R. & Co., at 81 per cent | 8,100 00 |
| | 6 | To $…,000 bought by Page, R. & Co., at 80¾ | 20,218 75 |
| | [illegible] | To $…,000, bought of S. Dillon, at 85 per cent | 51,850 00 |
| | [illegible] | To $…,000, bought of Page, R. & Co., 80¼ | 33,915 00 |
| | [illegible] | To $11,000 bought of Page, R. & Co., 80¾ | 8,896 25 |
| | 10 | To $…,000, bought of Oliver Ames, 85 | 218,450 00 |
| | [illegible] | To $…,000 bought of C. H. McCormick, 85 | 29,900 00 |
| | [illegible] | To $…,000 bought of Oakes Ames, 85 | 18,450 00 |
| | 14 | To $13,000 bought of R. G. Hazard, 85 | 11,050 00 |
| | [illegible] | To $12,000, bought of F. Nickerson, 85 | 10,200 00 |
| | 17 | To $5,000, bought of J. B. Johnston, 85 | 4,250 00 |
| | 19 | To $…,000 bought of F. W. Andrews, 81¼, Jan. 4 | 6,500 00 |
| | 19 | To $1,000 bought of B. F. Ham, 85 | 850 00 |
| | [illegible] | To $6,000 bought of B. F. Ham, 85 | 5,100 00 |
| | [illegible] | To $5,000 bought of W. H. Macy, 85 | 4,250 00 |
| | [illegible] | To $4,000 bought of J. N. Smith, 85 | 3,400 00 |
| | [illegible] | To $…,000 charged contractors as delivered E. W. Gilmore, and taken | 3,000 00 |
| | [illegible] | To … F. W. Andrews and returned Dec. 21 | 8,000 00 |
| | [illegible] | To exchange with Thomas … | 2,000 00 |
| | [illegible] | To $…,000 bought of J. Nickerson, … per cent | 12,500 00 |
| | [illegible] | To $…,000 bought of E. W. Gilmore, … per cent | 20,400 00 |
| | [illegible] | To $…,000 bought of John Duff, 81¼ | 60,937 50 |
| | [illegible] | To exchange with … | 18,000 00 |
| | [illegible] | To $…,000, of E. Atkins, at … per cent | 8,500 00 |
| | [illegible] | To $…,000 of Page, Richardson & Co. | 3,000 00 |
| | [illegible] | To first mortgage bonds | [illegible],000 00 |
| | | To discount on bonds bought: | |
| | | Jan. 4, of F. W. Andrews $…,000 at …¼ per cent | 1,500 00 |
| | | Jan. 7, Sidney Dillon $…,000 at … per cent | 9,150 00 |

| | | | |
|---|---|---|---|
| | [illegible] | [illegible] | [illegible] |
| | 23 | do | [illegible] |
| | 24 | do | [illegible] |
| | 26 | do | [illegible] |
| | 27 | do | [illegible] |
| | 28 | do | [illegible] |
| | 29 | do | [illegible] |
| | 30 | do | [illegible] |
| May | 14 | By H. … Crane, … treasurer | [illegible] |
| | 16 | do | [illegible] |
| | [illegible] | do | [illegible] |
| | [illegible] | do | [illegible] |
| | 30 | do | [illegible] |
| May | 1 | By W. J. Glidden, chairman | [illegible] |
| | 3 | do | [illegible] |
| | 4 | do | [illegible] |
| | 5 | do | [illegible] |
| | 6 | do | 41,000 00 |
| | 7 | do | [illegible],000 00 |
| | 8 | do | 111,000 00 |
| | 10 | do | 11,000 00 |
| | 11 | do | 44,000 00 |
| | 12 | do | 13,000 00 |
| | 13 | do | 310,000 00 |
| | 14 | do | 102,000 00 |
| | 15 | do | 16,000 00 |
| | 17 | do | 30,000 00 |
| | 21 | do | 39,000 00 |
| | 25 | do | 8,000 00 |
| | 27 | do | 40,000 00 |
| | 29 | do | 10,000 00 |
| | 31 | do | [illegible],000 00 |
| June | 4 | do | 10,000 00 |
| | [illegible] | By W. J. Glidden, chairman | 15,000 00 |
| | 9 | do | 8,000 00 |
| | 10 | do | [illegible],000 00 |

*First-mortgage bonds.—Abstract Ledger C.*

| Dr. | | | | | | |
|---|---|---|---|---|---|---|
| 1872. | | | | 1872. | | Cr. |
| Oct. 4 | To Sidney Dillon | $24,000 00 | | June 29 | By balance from Ledger B | $27,237,000 00 |
| | | | | | Balance to credit of bond account Jan. 31, 1873 | 27,213,000 00 |

[ROLLINS 17c.]

*Land-grant bonds.—Abstract Ledger B.*

| | | | | | |
|---|---|---|---|---|---|
| 1869. | | | 1869. | | |
| July 31 | To R. G. Hazard | $210,000 00 | April 23 | By H. C. Crane, assistant treasurer | $94,000 00 |
| [illegible]. 14 | To F. W. Andrews | 8,000 00 | 27 | ......do | 100,000 00 |
| 26 | To land-department | 263,000 00 | 27 | ......do | 140,000 00 |
| 23 | To contractors | 100,000 00 | 16 | By W. T. Glidden, chairman | 7,000 00 |
| [illegible] | ......do | 12,000 00 | 21 | ......do | [illegible]0,000 00 |
| | ......do | 14,000 00 | 21 | ......do | 51,000 00 |
| | To land-department | 58,000 00 | 22 | ......do | 10,000 00 |
| | ......do | 24,000 00 | 23 | ......do | 44,000 00 |
| | To O. F. Davis, land-agent | 39,000 00 | 24 | ......do | 1,190,000 00 |
| | | | 26 | ......do | 77,000 00 |
| | | | 27 | ......do | 178,000 00 |
| [illegible] | To 3 bonds delivered E. W. Gilmore and charged contractors—not taken | 3,000 00 | 28 | ......do | 357,000 00 |
| | | | 29 | ......do | 31,000 00 |
| 31 | To [illegible] bonds delivered F. W. Andrews and charged contractors, returned December 24 | 8,000 00 | 30 | ......do | 139,000 00 |
| | | | May 27 | By H. C. Crane, assistant treasurer | 309,000 00 |
| 28 | To bonds taken in payment for land in January by O. F. Davis, agent | 23,000 00 | 28 | ......do | 330,000 00 |
| | | | 30 | ......do | 10,000 00 |
| 28 | To bonds taken in payment for land in February by O. F. Davis, agent | 8,000 00 | 31 | ......do | 537,000 00 |
| [illegible]ch 31 | To bonds taken in payment for land in March by O. F. Davis agent | 40,000 00 | 1 | By W. T. Glidden, chairman | 225,000 00 |
| | | | 3 | ......do | 28,000 00 |
| 30 | To bonds taken in payment for lands in April by O. F. Davis, agent | 20,000 00 | 4 | ......do | 4,000 00 |
| | | | 5 | ......do | 50,000 00 |
| | To bonds taken in payment for land in May by O. F. Davis, agent | 23,000 00 | 6 | ......do | 91,000 00 |
| | | | 7 | ......do | 387,000 00 |
| | [illegible]onds taken in payment for land in June by O. F. Davis, [illegible]t | 23,000 00 | 8 | ......do | 78,000 00 |
| | | | 10 | ......do | 38,000 00 |
| | [illegible]s taken in payment for land in July by O. F. Davis, | 40,000 00 | 11 | ......do | 91,000 00 |
| | [illegible]s taken in payment for land in August by O. F. Da[illegible] | 35,000 00 | 12 | ......do | 65,000 00 |
| | [illegible]aken in payment for land in September by O. F. [illegible] agent | 16,000 00 | 13 | ......do | 140,000 00 |
| | [illegible]taken in payment for land in October by O. F. Da[illegible] | | 14 | ......do | 108,000 00 |
| | | | 15 | ......do | 16,000 00 |
| | | | 17 | ......do | 13,000 00 |
| | | | 20 | ......do | 55,000 00 |
| | | | 22 | ......do | 84,000 00 |

was the proceeds of bonds and stocks sold by him, and for which he received stock of the Union Pacific Railroad Company at par.

Q. Then deducting from the amount of stock given by you as above, $6,368,334.90, would show the amount of stock received on account of the profits as shown by these balance-sheets?—A. It would show the amount taken under the eleventh section of the contract. They subscribed for so much stock on account of the excess received from the bonds on account of construction.

Q. The aggregate profits made on the Ames and Davis contracts, as shown by the balance-sheets, exhibited with Mr. Crane's testimony, are $37,657,095. Now, state how much of that was bonds, how much stock, and how much money.—A. They received on account of the contract, $3,777,000 first mortgage bonds, amounting to $3,399,300; 4,400,000 certificates for first-mortgage bonds, which were afterward converted into income-bonds, amounting to $4,425,000; 5,841 income-bonds, amounting to $3,486,600, and subscribed for 240,000 shares of stock, amounting to $24,000,000; the balance was received in cash, $2,346,195.

Q. Have there been any payments made to the Credit Mobilier since the resolution of the directors fixing the amount due to the Credit Mobilier?—A. Not on that account.

Q. Have there been any payments made on any account?—A. Yes.

Q. On what account?—A. On current account.

Q. What does it have reference to?—A. It has reference to nothing particular. It is simply a current account, "paid them so much money on account."

Q. Does the Credit Mobilier have any other account?—A. It has two accounts; one with the balance due on the Hoxie contract that has never been paid.

Q. Nothing been paid on that?—A. No, sir.

Q. Look at the books of the Union Pacific Railroad and see what appears to be the cost of the whole road as shown by these books.—A. The whole cost, as appears from the books of the company, is $114,033,728.52, an itemized statement of which is herewith submitted, [marked "Ham 1."] Now, I would like to state the actual cost of building the Pacific Railroad as I make it up from the books of the contractors and books of the company. The actual cost is $71,208,399.18.

Q. What do you mean when you say the actual cost?—A. I mean the amount of money expended in building, losses on securities, discount, and interest, and other things which go to make up the cost of the road.

Q. In this account that you have presented I find an item of $2,581,180.09, discount and interest. Will you explain that?—A. That was interest on the money borrowed.

Q. From whom?—A. From outside parties, principally; some from inside parties.

Q. In what way was that money borrowed?—A. Some of it on demand loans and some of it on notes.

Q. Is there on the books of the company an account of that?—A. Yes, sir.

Q. State on what book and commencing at what page this discount and interest account may be found?—A. On ledger A, com page 585.

Q. Where will the journal entries be found?—A. Jus here.

Q. They will be on journals a[illegible] ks corr paging that is indicated on th

Q. What do I understand

Q. Did you ever keep any memoranda that would throw any light upon that subject?—A. I did at the time; but they are all gone now.

Q. How did you keep these memoranda?—A. I kept a bond-book, showing the number of each bond, and what was its disposition; where it was temporarily, and what was its final disposition.

Q. Where is that bond-book?—A. I do not know whether it is in the office or not.

Q. Is it not possible that these bonds may be out somewhere where they have been hypothecated?—A. No, sir; the coupons come in regularly.

Q. I suppose the coupons may come back; but the bonds do not find their way back?—A. No, sir; we have attempted by the coupons to trace the bonds back, but we find that parties having control of the bonds very often shifted numbers—mixed them up with their own bonds—and then they got shifted around elsewhere. We cannot tell anything about it.

---

NEW YORK, *February* 8, 1873.

EDWARD MORGAN sworn and examined.

By the CHAIRMAN:

Question. Where do you reside and what is your occupation?—Answer. I reside at 328 Fifth Avenue, New York City. Am a banker, of banking-house of M. Morgan & Sons, doing business No. 39 William street, New York City.

Q. What, if anything, do you know of three drafts drawn by J. M. S. Williams, treasurer of the Union Pacific Railroad Company, March 9, 1871, one for $20,626.45, one for $43,841.09, and one for $18,032.46? State all you know in relation to them.—A. They were drawn for account of C. S. Bushnell against land-grant bonds of the Union Pacific Railroad Company, at 70 cents to the dollar, and accrued interest. The proceeds of the drafts went to Mr. Bushnell's account on our books, and he got the benefit of the same. The drafts came to us on the 10th of March, 1871, were paid that day, and the bonds accompanied the drafts. The drafts and bonds I think were brought to us by Mr. Bushnell in person. That is all I know about the transaction.

Q. Do your books show anything in relation to a draft for $2,500, favor of E. H. Rollins, drawn by Mr. Bushnell?—A. Our books show that on the 10th of March, 1871, we paid Mr. Bushnell's draft, favor of E. H. Rollins, for $2,500.

---

NEW YORK, *February* 8, 1873.

THOMAS P. GILMAN sworn and examined.

By the CHAIRMAN:

Question. Where do you reside and what is your occu[illegible]
swer. Palisades, Rockland County, New York. Am a[illegible]
firm of Gilman, Son & Co., doing business in the [illegible]
47 Exchange Place.

Q. Look at this check, dated [illegible]
iams, treasurer, on Nation[illegible]
for $24,500, payable to th[illegible]
Spence, payable to order [illegible]
Rollins, secreta[illegible]

Q. Were you at a meeting of the board of directors of the Union Pacific Railroad Company, held in the city of Boston, March 9, 1871, and if so, do you know anything in relation to a claim of $126,000 that was considered by a committee at that meeting?—A. I was at the meeting on the 9th of March, and knew that the subject of compensation or allowance to Mr. Bushnell was placed in the hands of a committee with power to do what in their judgment was right to be done. And as president of the company, I was ex officio called on as a member of that committee. The committee heard Mr. Bushnell's claims, as stated by myself, and granted him the amount of $126,000, which was paid to him by the company. Mr. Bushnell stated that he was under great embarrassment on account of the company by undertaking to carry through himself and his associates large amounts of the securities very much above ruling market rates, and that he had, at sacrifice to his own business, given the company's interests at Washington a great deal of time and attention, and that he had called General Dodge there to aid him, and had agreed to pay him liberally for his time and expenses, all of which he wanted to carry out in good faith, and that if the company were willing to aid him reasonably he felt that he could go on and carry out every obligation he had made to the company. I knew of my own knowledge that Mr. Bushnell had been carrying a very large load of obligations, and for the various reasons given by Mr. Bushnell, the committee agreed that the company's interest and Mr. Bushnell's would be equitably served by granting the sum they did, and it was so paid to him.

Q. What securities was he carrying to which you have referred in your last answer, and who were his associates?—A. He was carrying a large amount of the land-grants and income-bonds of the company, that were taken by himself and associates in order to place the company in reasonable financial condition by providing for its interest due in January, and to provide money to lift and pay off the floating debt of the company. I had made this a condition before agreeing to accept the presidency, that all its old complications with the Credit Mobilier, unadjusted floating debt, and other questions of that character, should either be actually paid off or placed in such condition as to relieve the company from embarrassment from that source. To accomplish this purpose, Mr. Bushnell and his associates agreed, as I afterward understood, to purchase from the company, very much above their current market-values, four or five millions of the bonds referred to, no doubt with the prospect on their part that the improved financial condition of the company, and the revived credit of the new organization, would ultimately relieve them from loss. But this they found to be a slow process and the load a heavy one. I do not know who the associates of Mr. Bushnell were, but I think they were bankers of New York and Boston. Mr. Bushnell finally and fully, as I believe, carried out all his obligations to the company, and its credit by these various movements was preserved intact, and all its obligations met at maturity.

Q. Did Mr. Bushnell pay to you any portion of this $126,000, and if so, what amount, and on what account?—A. I had said to Mr. Bushnell, on several occasions, that I wanted very much to have moneys that I had advanced him restored to me as soon as he could; and after the committee had acted on the 9th of March, I said to him then that I hoped he could give me a portion [illegible] moneys he owed me. He paid me the least amount I could [illegible] with that day, and I [illegible]teen or twenty thousand dollars [illegible], as I think, at this [illegible] edge on the subject. The Government directors relied altogether on Mr. Williams, having full confidence in whatever he said.

Q. I find, in a report made by you and other Government directors, dated at New York, January 7, 1867, that you speak of the track of this road as laid three hundred and five miles from Omaha, and the necessary engines, cars, and stations furnished for immediate use, although not fully equipped; that the road has been accepted from the contractors, and steps taken for a settlement at $50,000 per mile, of which $5,000 per mile was for equipment, under the provisions of the Hoxie contract, referred to in your report of July 8, 1865, and you say: "The said contract was extended to the one hundredth meridian of longitude, by the executive committee, without the knowledge of any of the Government directors, the extension of the said contract not having been reported to the board of directors till October last. Such action, however, had been taken by the company as rendered the contract legally binding." What objection was made, if any, to the extension of the Hoxie contract to the one hundredth meridian; and what was the ground of objection taken on the part of the Government directors?—A. At the first meeting of the Government directors with the board, in New York, in the fall of 1864, the Hoxie contract came to our knowledge, having been executed by the board previous to our appointment. We then condemned it. That was as early as 1864, when the contract was only for one hundred miles west of Omaha. We condemned it, but under the circumstances, considering that it was made while the war was still existing, considering the high price of labor, and the want of means to transport iron and other materials to Omaha, except up the Missouri River, which was an uncertain way, and considering the consequently enhanced cost of materials, we concluded that we would simply protest against the contract in our report to the Secretary of the Interior, and let it go. But afterward, when we discovered that the executive committee had extended that contract 150 miles farther, without submitting it to the board, and without communicating or reporting it to the board, for nearly a year afterward, we did feel disposed to protest and to take some action on the subject. But why we did not, I cannot give the reasons now. We felt outraged at the time.

Q. What was the ground of that objection?—A. That the price was too large, too extravagant; it was $50,000 a mile, but it should not have cost the half of that. That was the ground of our objection.

Q. It is stated also in this report of yours that "it is expected that the Cedar Rapids and Missouri Railroad will be completed the present month through Western Iowa, which will save much expense, with more certainty in future for the transportation of materials." Do you recollect whether that completion was in fact effected as then expected?—A. I think it was.

Q. What effect had that facility of transportation on the construction of the Union Pacific Railroad?—A. It cheapened it very much, and rendered more certain the transportation of materials.

Q. When did you leave the direction?—A. In July, 1867, I think.

Q. In your report of March 2, 1867, I see this statement: "At a regular meeting of the board of directors just closed a contract was concluded for the construction of two hundred and twelve miles of the line extending from the present terminus to the base of the Rocky Mountains, at $42,000 and $45,000 per mile, which includes provision for ample equipment and stations." With whom was that contract made, and from what point?—A. [illegible] Three hundred and five miles [illegible] e hundredth meridian. I think the one hundredth meridian ndred and forty-seven miles west of Omaha.

n this two hundred and twelve miles would begin some fifty- west of the one hundredth meridian and extend to the base ocky Mountains?—A. Yes.

te what amount of money during your connection with the paid in on the stock of the Union Pacific Railroad Com-.. I do not think that there was more than $200,000 or $250,000, 10 per cent. (whichever it was) that the charter required. We d that Dr. Durant furnished the money to build the road be-aha, (for the first thirty or forty miles beyond Omaha it was a ensive road,) and that he got that expensive part about fin-n his own private means and with the money which the stock-paid in, and then the Credit Mobilier began to appear. But why it appeared was kept as much concealed from the Gov-directors as it could possibly be. We were not admitted to nfidence. But we knew that the road was carried on with an hich none of us ever saw before, and it was perfectly satis- us as representing the Government on that board.

or to the beginning of 1867, was the road, so far as you knew, mically constructed, and were its affairs as economically ad-d, as could reasonably be expected under the circumstances?—k so, fully. The road was constructed in a very economical but, at the same time, in a permanent manner. The sub-con-re let with a good deal of care and a good deal of cutting down so that the sub-contractors made but a fair profit.

re you personally acquainted with the manner in which the ions to the stock of the company were paid in, and with the n which dividends were made to the parties connected with ruction or with the government of the road prior to your leav-lirection?—A. No, sir; I cannot say that I have any personal on. We were aware that there was but little stock subscribed out little money arising from the stock, and there certainly was nd on the Union Pacific Railroad stock. We were kept ignorant hing that the Credit Mobilier did. We did not wish to acquire mation in regard to it. In fact, from what little information to our knowledge we entered a protest against their proceed-

ish to state to you the prices at which the Oakes Ames con- let:

| | Per mile. |
|---|---|
| 100 miles | $42,000 |
| ection, 167 miles | 45,000 |
| :tion, 100 miles | 96,000 |
| ection, 100 miles | 80,000 |
| tion, 100 miles | 90,000 |
| :tion, 100 miles | 90,000 |

ng to 667 miles in all, and extending from the one hundredth meri-tward. State, from your knowledge of the surveys then made rted to the board, as to the general character of the route, also f transportation, and of the condition of the country, and ' 'n the possession of the company, how these fr. Ames, would, in your judgment, com- t price for the work.—A. From the tor of the road, from the surveys of the condition of the country out

Q. Can you tell us within a hundred shares the interest you had in that Contract and Finance Company?—A. Really, I never saw the subscription list.

Q. And have no idea of how much you had?—A. Really, I have no idea; and I do not know what the capital stock is. I believe it is five millions.

Q. How many stockholders were there, as nearly as you can recollect?—A. I do not think I ever heard.

Q. Who were the principal stockholders in that Contract and Finance Company?—A. I do not know that, for I never saw the list.

Q. Were you present when the contract was made with that Contract and Finance Company?—A. No, sir.

Q. Had you anything to do with that contract?—A. Not that I recollect. I have been on this side. I have been here for eleven years, almost all the time.

Q. By whom were the contracts made on the part of the Central Pacific Railroad Company to build this road?—A. The Central Pacific Railroad Company, I suppose, would represent the one side, and the Contract and Finance Company the other side.

Q. I want to know who were representing the Central Pacific Railroad Company in making these contracts. Did you have an executive committee, a contracting committee, or in what way was it done?—A. I do not know; I have not been in California probably (except for a few days at a time) in eleven years, and I never looked into these matters.

Q. Do you know what the net earnings of the Central Pacific Railroad Company are now?—A. I do not know. I can make a statement. The figures are easily obtained.

Q. Do you know what its present indebtedness is?—A. My impression is that the Central Pacific Railroad Company owes little or nothing outside of its bonded debt. We have taken great pains to make the Central Pacific Railroad a solid, paying road. Wherever we could run branches to advance the interest of the main road we have done so. I have attended to matters on this side, and can tell you pretty much all that has taken place on this side, but very little of the other side.

Q. Do you know what the floating indebtedness of the company is?—A. My impression is that we may say we have no floating debt. We may have a small floating debt, but it is covered by cash, or by something equivalent to cash.

Q. What has been done by the Central Pacific Railroad Company in the way of consolidation with other roads?—A. There is the California and Oregon road; there is the San Joaquin Valley road, and there is the Western Pacific road.

Q. And the Southern Pacific?—A. No; that is another organization entirely. It runs into another system of roads. There is the Oakland road, I think, and there is the Alameda road.

Q. Are those roads now all under the direction of the Central Pacific Railroad Company?—A. Yes.

Q. And all controlled by the parties who control the Central Pacific Railroad?—A. I believe they are.

Q. Was the stock of those roads purchased by the persons who control the Central Pacific Railroad?—A. That was done by consolidation. It would naturally be by consolidation.

Q. Are there any ferries connected with any of those roads?—A. My impression is that those ferries at Oakland belong to the Central Pacific Railroad Company.

Q. Was he a director at that time?—A. I think not.

Q. Was he a stockholder?—A. I suppose so.

Q. Was Mr. E. B. Crocker a director or a stockholder, or both?—A. My impression is that he was a director: and you have to be a stockholder to be a director, as I understand the law.

Q. At what date was the contract made for constructing a portion of this road by the corporation styled "The Contract and Finance Company?"—A. I could not say.

Q. How much of the line of the road did the first contract which they took cover?—A. I could not answer that.

Q. Answer as near as you can.—A. I do not know. My impression is that the Finance Company built about six hundred miles of the road.

Q. You said it was nearly impossible to let that road, except in large tracts; was that true at the date of this letting—the first letting of the contract to the Finance Company?—A. Yes, sir. I think that the committee will see that it would have been impossible when they understand the circumstances under which the road was built. The Union Pacific people were pushing on with fearful speed and reckless expenditure to drive us out of the Salt Lake Valley—to drive us out of that business. We did not expect to have any local business on the four hundred miles of the eastern portion of our road, although I am happy to say it has since been developed and proves to be very satisfactory. We felt very anxious to have the road reach the Salt Lake Valley, so as to participate in that trade, and we thought it a vital point that the road should be pushed on to meet the Union Pacific about where we did meet it. I made an overland trip across the continent of thirteen hundred miles in the winter to see how they were getting along. They were moving camps, paying double wages, &c.

Q. At the formation of this constructing company, what proportion of the stock of the Central Pacific road was owned by the persons that became members of the Contract and Finance Company?—A. I have no idea.

Q. Was it half?—A. I have no idea at all.

Q. Can you not approximate?—A. No, I could not. I never saw the books.

Q. Do you know what amount of stock had been issued at this particular date, November, 1867?—A. No, I do not.

Q. Another averment in the bill from which I have read to you is, that after the organization of the Contract and Finance Company, all the contracts made and entered into in the name of the Central Pacific Railroad Company for materials to be furnished and for work to be done were by Leland Stanford, Charles Crocker, and their confederates, composing a majority of the directors of the Central Pacific Railroad Company, voted to be let, and were in fact let, and entered into by the Central Pacific Railroad Company of the one part and the Contract and Finance Company of the other part, without advertising the same, and without in any manner inviting competition therefor. Now, the first question I desire to ask you is, whether at that date you had any personal knowledge of that first letting to the Contract and Finance Company?—A. My impression is that I did not know anything about it at that date.

Q. Tell me whether you were in California at the period of the letting.—A. There was three years that I was not in Californi[illegible] if I recollect correctly, from about 1863 to 1866.

Q. Were you present at any meeting or i[illegible] to the formation or organization of this C[illegible]

By the CHAIRMAN:

Q. Do you embrace in the operating expenses the cost of maintaining the road?—A. Most assuredly.

Q. And the renewal of iron?—A. Yes.

By Mr. SHELLABARGER:

Q. You do not include in it the laying of new track for any considerable distance?—A. We have done so thus far. I suppose that this year we put in twenty miles of iron rail here and there, piecing up. This goes into the operating expenses.

Q. You include, then, in your statement of a little over 40 per cent. for operating expenses, this renewing of the track with steel rails?—A. No, not the steel rails, but the renewal of the track with iron rails. I presume the steel rail has gone into the construction account.

By Mr. HOAR:

Q. I understood you to say that there has as yet been no dividend paid by the Central Pacific Railroad Company to its stockholders?—A. That is the answer I gave.

Q. Is it not your belief that the persons who have been prominent in the management of the Central Pacific Railroad Company, including yourself, received considerable values either in moneys, bonds, or stock, as profits on contracts made for its construction?—A. I do not think we have made as much as we would have made if we had not gone into the road.

Q. I ask you if it is not your belief that persons active in the management of the Central Pacific Railroad Company, including yourself, received considerable values (I do not ask whether they were reasonable or unreasonable) as profits on contracts for its construction?—A. I think we have. I think I have an interest in a contract of the Contract and Financial Company, and I think I have made some money.

Q. Do you mean to have me understand, by the mode in which you answer that question, that any doubt exists in the mind of yourself that you have received yourself, while an officer of the Central Pacific Railroad Company, considerable values, either in money, bonds, or stocks, as profits upon contracts made for its construction?—A. I think I have. I have received no money.

Q. The question I now put to you is, whether you mean the committee to understand from the way in which you make that answer that you have any doubt on that subject in your mind?—A. I am not so clear as I would like to be.

Q. Be good enough to attend to my question. Have you any doubt in your mind that you have received considerable values, while a stockholder and officer of the Central Pacific Railroad Company, as profits on contracts made for its construction?—A. If I have received them at all it is as a stockholder in the Contract and Finance Company.

Q. I do not care whether you have received them as your share of the profits made by a company of which you were a member, but simply whether you have received as profits on contracts made for its construction considerable values?—A. I think I have.

Q. Have you any doubt of it?—A. I have doubts about [illegible] but I presume I have some paper stock. If there have [illegible] made by my partner I have got some of them.

Mr. HOAR. I am going to put that questior [illegible] to give a frank answer to it.

The WITNESS. I will endeav[illegible]

parties?—A. My impression is that it was. I should like to say that I spoke to a good many people to go into that road, and almost every person refused to do so; and we had great trouble in getting people.

Q. Does your company have agencies in the principal Atlantic cities, or any of them, to make contracts for freight and to look after its freight interests?—A. We have a man in New York.

Q. Do you have any connection with that—any supervision?—A. No, sir; that is under the superintendent.

Q. Does your company have a treasurer or a treasury in New York?—A. No.

Q. Where does it pay its interest?—A. At Fisk & Hatch's, in New York.

Q. Do you have any supervision of that?—A. I generally look after it.

Q. How much looking after does it require on your part?—A. Well, I see that the money is there to pay the interest.

Q. Twice a year?—A. Yes, sir.

Q. The money is sent from California?—A. Yes, sir.

Q. What are the matters on this side which you say you attend to?—A. Well, I attend to buying all material. Every day I get orders from California.

Q. Material for the maintenance of the road?—A. I just got an order yesterday for ten locomotives.

Q. I do not care to go into details. I see that is an important duty. Now what other duty do you attend to besides buying material?—A. I am president of the Chesapeake and Ohio road.

Q. I do not mean other business. You describe your office as attending to matters on this side. I want to know generally what you attend to?—A. I do not think of anything else.

Q. Are there any other officers or servants of the road on this side except yourself, the freight agents, and the men who pay this money to the bondholders?—A. No, sir; there are no other agents on this side.

Q. What is the salary of the president?—A. I think it is $10,000.

Q. What is the salary of the treasurer?—A. I think it is $10,000.

Q. And of the vice-president?—A. I think it is $10,000. It is credited to me out there, and I draw upon it from time to time. It was $10,000 a year, and I suppose it is that yet.

Q. Do you have a compensation or commission in addition to your salary for the purchase of these materials?—A. The last monthly statement I sent out to California was one million and odd dollars. I send out every month a statement and they take it and put it on their books, and I have never made one shilling out of it as percentage or commission.

Q. I am not directing any inquiry which has for it the purpose of investigating whether you have dealt honestly with the company or whether you have been improperly paid. I do not mean to suggest that there is any doubt in my mind about your honesty. I simply want to know whether, in addition to this salary of vice-president, whatever it may be, you have employment for the road which warrants the payment to you of a commission or a percentage?—A. No, sir: there is none. I never got one cent commission from the road.

Q. What are the duties of Mr. Franchot?—A. Well, if you will all me, he acts——

Q. In the first place his duties, as I understand, are sub you—that is, they are conducted under your general direct sir.

Q. Now, what are the duties?

| Names. | Stock Credit Mobilier of America. | Dividend in stock Union Pacific Company. | Dividend in cash. | Signatures. |
|---|---|---|---|---|
| | *Shares.* | | | |
| John L. King | 100 | $40 00 | $6,000 00 | [2-cent rev. stamp.] |
| C. A. Lombard | 100 | 40 00 | 6,000 00 | Do. |
| LeGrand Lockwood | 500 | 200 00 | 30,000 00 | Do. |
| A. A. Low | 100 | 40 00 | 6,000 00 | Do. |
| Wm. H. Macy | 300 | 120 00 | 18,000 00 | Do. |
| H. S. McComb | 1,250 | 500 00 | 75,000 00 | Do. |
| Cyrus H. McCormick | 943 | 377 20 | 56,580 00 | Do. |
| Robert G. S. McNeil | 5 | 2 00 | 300 00 | Do. |
| E. C. Moore | 10 | 4 00 | 600 00 | Do. |
| Charles Neilson | 150 | 60 00 | 9,000 00 | Do. |
| Frederick Nickerson | 250 | 100 00 | 15,000 00 | Do. |
| Joseph Nickerson | 330 | 132 00 | 19,800 00 | Do. |
| Thomas Nickerson | 150 | 60 00 | 9,000 00 | Do. |
| George Opdyke | 712 | 284 80 | 42,720 00 | Do. |
| Nathan Peck | 100 | 40 00 | 6,000 00 | Do. |
| J. B. Pigot | 150 | 60 00 | 9,000 00 | Do. |
| Paul Pohl, jr | 6 | 2 40 | 360 00 | Do. |
| Joseph Richardson | 50 | 20 00 | 3,000 00 | Do. |
| Henry A. Robbins | 100 | 40 00 | 6,000 00 | Do. |
| Royal E. Robbins | 300 | 120 00 | 18,000 00 | Do. |
| Harvey Sanford | 125 | 50 00 | 7,500 00 | Do. |
| J. H. Scranton | 5 | 2 00 | 300 00 | Do. |
| F. Skinner & Co | 250 | 100 00 | 15,000 00 | Do. |
| F. Skinner & Co., trustees. | 250 | 100 00 | 15,000 00 | Do. |
| J. N. Smith | 405 | 162 00 | 24,300 00 | Do. |
| Thomas M. Stetson | 30 | 12 00 | 1,800 00 | Do. |
| W. B. Stevens, trustee | 50 | 20 00 | 3,000 00 | Do. |
| B. D. Stewart | 5 | 2 00 | 300 00 | Do. |
| Isaac Thatcher | 92 | 36 80 | 5,520 00 | Do. |
| Lydia Torrey | 11 | 4 40 | 660 00 | Do. |
| Willie Davis Train | 175 | 70 00 | 10,500 00 | Do. |
| Ezekiel Trowbridge | 50 | 20 00 | 3,000 00 | Do. |
| Henry Trowbridge | 75 | 30 00 | 4,500 00 | Do. |
| Sophia Vernon | 1 | 40 | 60 00 | Do. |
| C. C. Waite | 80 | 32 00 | 4,800 00 | Do. |
| J. M. S. Williams | 620 | 248 00 | 37,200 00 | Do. |

Dividend of R. G. Hazard was receipted for by R. G. Hazard, attorney.
Dividend of I. P. Hazard was receipted for by R. G. Hazard, attorney.
Dividend of R. Hazard was receipted for by R. G. Hazard, attorney.
Dividend of Elizabeth Hazard was receipted for by R. G. Hazard, attorney.
Dividend of Elizabeth Hazard, trustee, was receipted for by R. G. Hazard, attorney.
Dividend of Mary P. Hazard, was receipted for by R. G. Hazard, attorney.
Dividend of Anna Hazard was receipted for by R. G. Hazard, attorney.
Dividend of Anna Horner was receipted for by R. G. Hazard, attorney.
Dividend of Lydia Torrey was receipted for by R. G. Hazard, attorney.
Dividend of Sophia Vernon was receipted for by R. G. Hazard, attorney.

STATE OF NEW YORK,
*City and County of New York, ss:*

I, Nathaniel Gill, a commissioner for the State of Rhode Island [illegible] for the city, county, and State of New York, duly commissioned [illegible] sworn, and dwelling in the city of New York, do hereby certify [illegible] have this day carefully examined and compared the foregoing [illegible] a certain instrument with the original instrument of which [illegible] to be a copy, and, after such examination and comparison [illegible] that [illegible] the [illegible] true and correct [illegible] [illegible] thereof, save [illegible]

ALLEY, JOHN B.—Continued.

held and for what purpose, 330; the Hoxie contract, its extent, &c., 331; track laid not accepted by the Government, 331; the Oakes Ames contract extended over the one hundred and thirty-eight miles of completed road, in order to give the Credit Mobilier a profit upon the construction of that portion of the road, 332; Credit Mobilier claimed an interest in the Ames contract, 333; don't know how the profits were estimated, 333; dividends, amount, dates, &c., 334; in case the money paid out in dividends was required to complete the road, it was to be paid back, 334, 335; loans made to the road, how secured, 335; dividends could only properly be made out of the earnings of the road, 336; actual cost for building the road under the Ames contract, 336, 337; $12,000,000 profit, 337, 338; Mr. Ames did not expect to put the contract through himself, 338; value of stock, 339; what saves the company from bankruptcy, 339, 340; large sums owing to the Credit Mobilier by the Union Pacific Railroad at the time of making the Ames contract, 340; road accepted by the Government, and bonds issued, with dates, &c., 341; consideration paid to Hoxie for the assignment of contract, 342; the road considered in a delicate position financially, 342, 343; amount of Union Pacific Railroad stock held by Mr. Alley, 344; statement, and additional testimony of Mr. Alley, 556.

AMES, OAKES, testimony of:

The Government has paid to the Union Pacific Railroad Company $16,000 per mile to the foot of the Rocky Mountains, p. 23; about $27,000,000 of bonds in the whole, 23; the Government has given about one-fourth of the land, and withholds the other three-fourths, 23; we have got the land certified to us for 250 miles at twenty sections to the mile, in all, 5,000 sections, 23; amount of the first-mortgage bonds prior to the lien of the United States, about $27,000,000, 23; first-mortgage bonds were used for the construction of the road, 23; the first mortgage-bonds sold at 92½, 23; the bonds were sold for 92½, and we afterward got par for them, 23; about $2,000,000 worth of land sold, 23, 24; the Credit Mobilier assumed the Hoxie contract, 24; the Union Pacific Railroad paid over $17,000,000 on the Ames contract, 24; price per mile paid, 25; the Boomer and Davis contracts were assigned to the trustees, 25; I think the entire cost for construction of the Union Pacific Railroad, including the equipment, and the entire paraphernalia of the road, amounted to about $50,000,000, 25; stock all paid in cash, 25; I think we made about 15 per cent. on the Ames contract, 26; the first-mortgage bonds were taken by the trustees, 26; I took the contract without regard to anybody else, 27; dividends paid, 27; Union Pacific Railroad is not now paying dividends, 27; Union Pacific Railroad earnings, 27; net proceeds last year over running expenses and interest on bonds, $3,500,000, 28; I am a shovel-maker, 28; I looked over the estimates before making the contract, 28; I estimated that I should make 20 per cent., 29; the profits of the Credit Mobilier were about 300 per cent., 29; I guaranteed lots o[illegible] [illegible] loss, 29; I guaranteed Senator Grimes and others, 29; I took [illegible] I made the contract, 30; my present judgment is, that w[illegible] [illegible] the Oakes Ames contract, 30; I think the pro[illegible] [illegible] must have been 300 per cent., but I cann[illegible] [illegible] $18,000 paid at Willard's, 344; I have [illegible] the chief engineer on the 31st of [illegible] [illegible] to the first president of the Union [illegible] [illegible] Dix was a stockholder befor[illegible] [illegible] there was a letter from Gene[illegible] [illegible] Painter was clerk to some [illegible] [illegible] the 16th day of October, 1867, [illegible] 723; I wish to correct my for[illegible] [illegible] the words "$16,000 a mile in st[illegible] [illegible] bonds," and on the same [illegible] substitute "the trustees;" also [illegible]

[illegible] October, 1866, p. 241; elected [illegible] became a stockholder in the [illegible] tract assigned to trustees [illegible] Oliver Ames president of [illegible] ver Ames one of th[illegible] signed, 242; O[illegible] [illegible] 242 [illegible]

AMES, OLIVER—Continued.

by Mr. Lambert in relation to the Hoxie contract, 283 and 284; Boomer contract, 285; responsibility of contractors, 285; bribe given to a Government commissioner, 287, 288, 289, and 290; trustees receive money on their contracts, [illegible]; stock wanted to control the road, 291; advice of counsel in regard to the issue of stock, 292; money paid to General B. F. Butler, 293; report of John J. Cisco relating to legal expenses, 295, 296, 297, 298, and 299; suspense account, 300 and 301; money paid to Hon. Thad. Stevens, 302 and 303.

ATKINS, ELISHA, testimony of:

Stockholder in the Credit Mobilier, 303; director Union Pacific Railroad Company, 303; I hold in my possession the note for $2,000,000, 304; the circumstances under which the $2,000,000 note was given stated, 304; copy of the note, 304; the note never was used, 304; the note was given as collateral security for the parties signing the bond, and for no other purpose, 304; a member of the finance committee, 305; the $126,000 for legal expenses, 305; suppose the $126,000 was spent legitimately, 306; the $50,000 for special legal expenses, 306; the $50,000 paid out under the direction of the president of the company, 306; reason for holding the $2,000,000 note stated, 306; names of the parties who signed the bond for which the $2,000,000 note was given as collateral, 306.

## B.

BUSHNELL, CORNELIUS S., testimony of:

Relation sustained to the Union Pacific Railroad Company, p. 38; first directors Union Pacific Railroad Company, 38; history of the transactions of the company, 38; how the construction of the road was commenced, 39; surveys made before the Hoxie contract, 39; rate at which the contract was let to Hoxie, 39; extension of the Hoxie contract, 39; there was only one letting made to Hoxie, 39; assignment of the Hoxie contract to the Credit Mobilier, 40; Hoxie to be paid in securities in the road, 40; amount received from the Government, with statement of Mr. Bushnell, 40; bonds given to the new stockholders to enlarge the stock of the Credit Mobilier, 40, 41; paying money to the Credit Mobilier secured bonds in the Union Pacific Railroad Company, 41; ten millions of bonds sold at 95, 42; the bonds were sold by the treasurer of the Union Pacific Railroad Company, 42; Black Hills line adopted in the spring of 1867, 43; the cost of building less than at first anticipated, 43; Ames contract let on actual surveys and location by the engineer, 43; reports of engineers, how made, 43; the residue of the construction to the western terminus was by Davis, 44; description of the road over the Rocky Mountains, 45; the road was completed on the 10th of May, 1869, 45; the Pacific Road meets promptly the interest on its bonds, 46; the average price of stock last year was 38, 47; the highest price paid for stock, 45¼ to 45½, 47; stock sold as low as $9 per share, 47; land-grant bonds outstanding upon unsold land, 48; cost of road, 48 and 49; mineral products from Salt Lake, 49; annual earnings of the road, 49; what the Government has saved by the road, 50; the engineer in charge representing Mr. Ames was Mr. Reed, 50; the Credit Mobilier had nothing to do with the construction of the road; it was done by the seven trustees, 50; estimates were only submitted to the trustees, 51; reports of the engineers, how and where kept, 51; average gross earnings of the road yearly, 52; effect upon the Union Pacific of the completion of the Northern and Southern Pacific Railroads, 52; amount of bonds issued by the Union Pacific Railroad, 53; contracts, by whom drawn, 53; names of the attorneys employed by the Union Pacific Company, 54; General Butler paid counsel fee, 55; no money paid to elect Harlan or any other Senator, 55; money contributed to aid in elections, 56, 57, 58; stock sold to members of Congress, 58, 59; stock guaranteed to subscribers, 59; when the stock subscribed for by Congressmen was paid, 60, 61; I was present at the meeting of the board of directors of the Union Pacific Railroad on the 9th of March, 1871, 528; I was one of the committee to investigate the account for $126,000, 528; no vouchers were presented, it was based on a statement of my own, 529; statement of Bushnell in relation to the $126,000, 529, 530; I gave Colonel Scott the $19,000 check, 531; I borrowed money from Ordway, 531; the persons to whom the $126,000 was paid, 532, 533; I was not aware that I was on the committee, 534; the $19,000 check was not given to Mr. Wilson, I received it and paid it over to Colonel Scott, 535; the first bridge-bonds issued were in the latter part of the year 1870, 536; the money raised on the bonds was seven or eight hundred thousand dollars, 536; I got the accommodation from the 28th to the 30th of December, 1870, 536; the bridge-bonds were issued under the general authority in the charter; the bonds were secured by a mortgage or a trust deed, 537; the bonds pledged as collaterals for a loan in New York, 537; two million five hundred thousand dollars in bridge-bonds, two million one hundred and thirty-six thousand

BARNES, OLIVER W.—Continued.

153; resolution to equalize the date of payment to increase stock subscriptions, 154; report of the treasurer to the stockholders of the Credit Mobilier, 154; list of stockholders of Credit Mobilier, May 18, 1866, 155; stock-list of the Credit Mobilier of America, May 17, 1867, 156; list of stockholders of the Credit Mobilier, May 16, 1868, 157; subscription-list to the Credit Mobilier, 159; increase of railway bureau, 160.

BONDS.

United States 6 per cent. 30-year bonds, 615; United States 6 per cent. 30-year bonds on hand, 616; United States 6 per cent. 30-year currency-bonds, 618; first-mortgage bonds, 619; Union Pacific Railroad bonds, 611; land-grant bonds, 624, 626, 627; income-bonds, 611, 627; income-bonds and stock sold by trustees, 634; bonds sold by trustees, 633; bonds of all classes, 630; balance-sheet, Ames contract, 633; balance-sheet, Davis contract, 633.

BUTLER, Hon. B. F., testimony of:

Letter from John B. Alley to General Butler, 683; General Butler's statement in regard to his connection with the Union Pacific Railroad, 683.

C.

CLARK, HORACE F., testimony of:

President of the Union Pacific Railroad, p. 394; elected president 6th of March, 1872; never was connected with the Credit Mobilier, 394; made report to the Secretary of the Interior 12th September, 1872; I only know the cost of the road from book-account, 394; the items that go to make up the capital stock of the company, 394; what the company owns, 395; the floating debt, in round numbers, is $2,000,000, 395; in the floating debt we do not embrace arrearages of interest due to the Government, 395; the floating debt is wholly in notes, 395; gross and net earnings of the road, 396; a detailed statement of the earnings, 396; if the Government withheld the money, and there should be a snow-blockade, I think the result would be disastrous to the road, 397; the weight of the iron per yard is 58 pounds, 397; no fund has been set apart for renewing the iron, 397; it is not customary for railroads to put aside a sinking-fund, 398; I think it will be necessary to expend this year half a million of dollars for relaying the track, 398; the cost for relaying is to be deducted from the gross earnings, 398; I have not had the practical management of any road, 399; have given attention to railroads, 399; unfriendly relations between railroads and the State or Federal Government would affect its prosperity, 400; I think there is no traffic that requires any very large expenditure, except for the maintenance of the track, 401; there have been "accommodation transactions" with the company since my administration, 402; those who have loaned the company money are secured by collaterals, 402; the stock, instead of being estimated at 100 cents to the dollar, was estimated at 30 cents, 403; coal was discovered while the road was in course of construction, 404; rumors about coal, 405; at the time of the Ames contract, I think the belief was quite universal that coal deposits accessible would be found, 405; where the first indications of coal appeared, 406; copy from Durant's report, 406; reports relating to coal, 407, 408; Evans Pass, 408; the general route of the road was understood before the Ames contract, 409; copy from the report of Mr. Dodge, 409; became a stockholder after the 1st of January, 1872, 410; not a cent used to carry elections, 410; an amount equivalent to the capital stock is sold over many times in the course of a year, 410; communications were sent to me, saying that there was danger of [illegible] being introduced that would injure the road, 410; copies of communication [illegible] answers, 411, 412, 413, 414, 415; resolution for the issuing of sixteen milli[illegible] bonds, 416; the bonds are being engraved, 416; the sales of the stock of [illegible] Pacific Railroad Company have been very large during the past year, [illegible] electing officers we give notice in advance, keep the books open [illegible] to permit transfers, then we close the books, 418; Hon. S. Shellab[illegible] to the witness a series of questions relating to the Ames and [illegible] which are fully answered on 418, 419, 420, 421, 422, 423, 424 [illegible] terrogatories propounded by Hon. G. F. Hoar, 425, 426 [illegible] 433, 434, 435; salaries paid the presidents of the road, [illegible] service, some service, while in France, 436; the sur[illegible] 436; after General Dix left the road he received $5[illegible] coal contract, 438, 439; there is no such thing as [illegible] the outlays for repairs will come out of the net [illegible] the assets of the company hypothecated, 441, 4[illegible] except the $2,000,000, 442; I do not think the [illegible]

CRANE, HENRY C.—Continued.

30 per cent., 630; extracts from the books of the company, 631; there were $5,811,000 income-bonds sold by the company to the trustees, at 60 cents, 631; balance-sheet, Ames contract, 632; income-bonds and stock sold by trustees, 636.

## D.

DEY, PETER A., testimony of:

I was employed in September, 1862, to make a reconnaissance from the Missouri River to Salt Lake, and tell what I thought of the chances of building a road, 238, 239; I was employed about the 1st of September, 1863, to make surveys, by Durant, 239; the Evans Pass was discovered in the fall of 1865; the grading is very light until you get to the Black Hills, 239; no estimate made prior to my connection with the road, 240; my idea is that the estimates were large, 240; Mr. John E. Henry instructed me to make a large estimate, 240; said he got his instructions from Durant, 240; I think $30,000 per mile for construction, including equipments, would cover all expenses on the road between Omaha and the one hundreth meridian, 241; estimate for the second hundred miles, 241; made the second estimate on the first one hundred miles September or October, 1864; I resigned as chief engineer Union Pacific Railroad 30th December, 1864, 668; I examined the whole line from Salt Lake Valley to Omaha, 668; my estimate was that the road could be built in cash for $40,000,000, 669; my resignation was tendered because I objected to being made an instrument to carry out the provisions of the Hoxie contract, 669; copy of Mr. Dey's letter of resignation, 669; resignation sent to General Dix, with copy of private letter from Dey to General Dix, 669; copy of reply sent by General Dix to Dey, 670, 671; my objections to the Hoxie contract were, that it was letting the work for $2,000,000 more than it ought to have been let, 671; my experience in railroad-building had been that in the early stages of a road it should not be burdened with debt, 671; from the terminus of the one hundred miles to the one hundredth meridian my figures were about $27,000 per mile, 672; I speak of cash when I speak of values, 673; I put on the prices that were ruling at that day, 674; the distance from the one hundredth meridian to the Black Hills about 270 miles, 674; no tunneling was necessary, 675; I never let a piece of work except on estimates, 675; instructions to increase estimate came through Durant, 676.

DICKEY, Hon. OLIVER J.:

Statement of Mr. Dickey, in defense of Hon. Thaddeus Stevens, 676.

DILLON, SIDNEY, testimony of:

Land owned by the Credit Mobilier at Council Bluffs, Iowa, 497; there has been a good deal of discussion about the initial point, 497; property owned by the Credit Mobilier at Council Bluffs, Iowa, Columbus, Nebraska, and a claim against the Union Pacific Railroad for $2,000,000, is about all the present property of the Credit Mobilier, 497; value of the lands, 497; a claim against the Union Pacific Railroad, as long as their note has never gone to protest, must be considered good, 498; in round numbers, I think the property of the Credit Mobilier is $2,200,000, 498; we have got a note of hand, but they claim that it is not a valid note, 498; if the depot was established at Council Bluffs, the land would be worth $400,000, 499; the Credit Mobilier holds less than 2,000 shares of the Union Pacific Railroad stock, 499; president of the Credit Mobilier since May, 1867, 499; I knew nothing about the transactions going on around Washington, or anywhere else, 500; I remember that J. M. S. Williams made a proposition to build the road, 500; the trustees got the stock and bonds which they divided up from the company, 502; there might have been an estimate made on the part which had been done by the Hoxie contract, 502; the highest grade on the road is ninety feet, 503; the contract was taken by Ames as an individual, 503; I am one of the seven trustees, 504; the checks were used to pay subscriptions of stock, 504; the bonds were procured in the same way, 504; the accounts between the Union Pacific Railroad and the trustees is about even, 505; I think I allowed Davis three or five thousand dollars for the assignment of his contract, 505; I don't think it would be a fraud if there was a small amount of work remaining to be done, 505; by getting the bonds a month or so sooner it would give us incr-
strength to build the next thirty or forty miles, 506; statement made by t[illegible]
president, Durant, 507; I think the Evans Pass was adopted as the ro[illegible]
date of the Oakes Ames contract, 508; it was impracticable to let the w[illegible]
quantities, 509; I thought we were doing justice to the Government, a[illegible]
had no right to complain, 510; T. C. Durant is a fast man, 510; I woul[illegible]
contract unless I thought I could make 20 per cent.

HAM, BENJAMIN F.—Continued.

Credit Mobilier, 10; books of the Credit Mobilier lost, 10; stock subscribed for in the Credit Mobilier, 11; my son holds three shares Credit Mobilier stock, 11; amount paid on account of the three shares of stock, 11; dividends received, 11; amount of Union Pacific Railroad stock received on three shares, 12; value of shares of Union Pacific Railroad stock received, 12; first directors of the Credit Mobilier, 13; list of officers of the Credit Mobilier, 13, 14; the Credit Mobilier had charge of building the road to the hundredth meridian, 14 the Credit Mobilier paid on account of construction under the Hoxie contract, $202,770, 14; the Credit Mobilier lost its money, 14; the Credit Mobilier lent money to the Union Pacific Railroad, simply on book account, 14; only one dividend declared by the Credit Mobilier, 15; Credit Mobilier stock increased, 15; value of the Credit Mobilier stock in 1867, 16; stock was held at all sorts of fictitious prices, 16; Credit Mobilier interest in the Ames contract, 16; at one time auditor of the Union Pacific Railroad Company, 16; was an officer of both corporations, 17; where the lost papers were contained, 17; lost books, 18; cause of their disappearance, 18; dates when stock in the Credit Mobilier was taken, with names of subscribers, 19; the profits on the Ames contracts were paid directly to stockholders, 20; only $5 or $10 per share paid on the stock, 20; stock, how issued, 21: at the time of making the Oakes Ames contract, the Credit Mobilier substantially owned all the stock of the Union Pacific Railroad, 21; of what the original stock consisted, 21; Union Pacific Railroad stock, $36,000,000; auditor of the Union Pacific Railroad, 371; the Hoxie contract cost $50,000 per mile, 371; the cost of the Hoxie contract, $14,290,835.90, 371; the $2,000,000 note referred to, 371; copies from the company's books showing items for cost of construction under the Hoxie contracts, 372, 373; what it cost the Credit Mobilier to build the road up to the one hundredth meridian, 373; copy of a letter written by Ham to Williams, 374; the cost of the Oakes Ames contract has never been settled, 374: the Credit Mobilier paid to the Union Pacific Railroad $1,111,670 and $4,000, 374: they paid it over in checks, 375; Credit Mobilier held 15,886 shares of 30 per cent. stock, 375; the $1,104,000 was paid over, by the trustees, to the Credit Mobilier, 375; the contractor subscribed for 22,960 shares of stock, 375; a check is considered cash, 375; the charter prohibited anything being taken for stock except cash, 375, 376; the amount paid on the Ames contract, 376: payments made on the Ames contract covered the whole extent of 667 miles, 377; Davis contract, 377: the amount of profit on the Hoxie contract, $6,272,232.91, 377: actual capital stock of the Credit Mobilier, 1st of January, 1867, 377; how the profits were disposed of, 377–382: the Credit Mobilier paid the Union Pacific Railroad 85 for the bonds, 383, 384: other stock divided in the regular dividends, 384; dividend made, 385; present assets of the Credit Mobilier, 385: whole amount of stock issued by the Union Pacific Railroad, $36,000,000, 386; how Rice paid for stock, 387; two dividends of 6 per cent, 15: resolution of Mr. Bushnell, that the treasurer pay over to the Credit Mobilier, in accordance with the provisions of the contract of Oakes Ames with the Union Pacific Railroad, of August 16, 1867, the sum of $1,104,000, or a sufficient sum to enable them to make the stock of the Union Pacific Railroad Company held by them full paid, 374: the Government bonds were sold at par, 636: the Ames contractors did not receive bonds, 636; statement of the cost of the Union Pacific Railroad to the company, 636: statement of the actual cost of the Union Pacific Railroad, 637; copy of a circular, 637: cost of the Hoxie contract, $12,974,416.24, 640; the above figures embrace the $1,994,769, 640; cost of the Hoxie contract to the contractors, 640; the Credit Mobilier advanced on the Ames contract, $576,697.01, 641; the profits made on the Ames and Davis contracts, how divided, 643: the aggregate profits made on the Ames and Davis contracts, 644; whole cost of the road, 644: well, it is the same thing, buying them or taking them upon a contract, 647.

HAY, ALEXANDER, testimony of:

I have retired from business, 457: I was in Washington pending the legislation of 1864, 457; received an order from Joseph B. Stewart on Durant to deliver me 230 construction bonds, which I received, 458: other bonds received, 458; I deposited the bonds with the president of the Merchants' National Bank of this city, to the credit of J. B. Stewart, 459; $18,000 was placed to my credit, 459: I am very intimate with J. B. Stewart, 460; I had almost daily transactions with Stewart, 461; I had no special business here in 1864, 461; I took an interest in endeavoring to get a bill reported to Congress, 461; Stewart paid me handsomely for what I did do, 462; he gave me $23,000, 462; I think there is a receipt for the 250 bonds in a trunk, 463; I was not a lawyer, 465.

ROLLINS, E. H.—Continued.

$14,550,278.91, 182; payment of $2,000,000, 182; consideration for which the $2,000,000 note was given, 182; additional charges on the Hoxie contract, 183; testimony relating to the $2,000,000 note, 183; an order to issue $16,000,000 additional bonds, 183; copy of preamble and resolutions, 184, 185; the $2,000,000 note and additional bond issue, 185; collateral security for the redemption of the bonds, 185; amount of bonds lost, 185; cost of the construction of the road covered by the Ames contract, 186; item charged to the Ames contract, 186; entry copied from the journal, 186; cost of the Davis contract, 187; copied from the books showing the cost of construction under the various contracts—Ames contract, Davis contract, and Hoxie contract, 187, 188; total cost of road to the Union Pacific Railroad Company, 188; amount of first-mortgage bonds issued by the Union Pacific Railroad Company, 188; land-grant bonds issued, 188; the Union Pacific Railroad Company does not owe the Credit Mobilier, 188; the Credit Mobilier indebted to the Union Pacific Railroad, 188, 189; present board of directors Union Pacific Railroad, 189; the company owes money to its directors, 189; special legal expenses, 189; resolution appointing a committee to audit legal expenses, 189, 190; testimony relating to legal expenses, including item of $126,000, 190, 191, 192, 193; the Union Pacific Railroad Company contract with the Pullman Car Company, 193, 194; the Harlan $10,000 legal-expense item of $126,000, and money to influence elections, 195; property belonging to the Union Pacific Railroad in the possession of the treasurer, 196; statement of assets, 197; loans in which the Union Pacific Railroad has an interest, 198, 199; net earnings for the last year $4,000,000, 199; the Government 5 per cent. comes in when the road is completed, 200; claim against the Government for transportation, 200; gross and net earnings, 200, 201; statement of the indebtedness of the Union Pacific Railroad, 210; statement of notes payable December 10, 1872, 210; notes due in January, 211; notes due in February, 211; notes due in March, 212; notes due in April, 212; demand notes, 212; statement of all the current indebtedness of the company, 212; Omaha bridge bonds, 212; the earnings on the bridge are ample to pay the interest on the bonds, 213; in favor of the Government recognizing the road as completed, 213; amount required to complete the road, 214; land-grant bonds, 214; the average price per acre for which lands were sold, $4.25, 214; the road will need for the present the same assistance it had in the past, 214, 215; estimated time that rails will last, from seven to ten years, 215; permanent counsel in the employ of the road, and salaries paid, 216; examined with reference to the $126,000, 216, 217; special attorneys employed, 218; corrected statement of Mr. Rollins, 219; the indenture under which the Omaha bridge bonds were issued bears date 1st day of November, A. D. 1870, 582; resolution in regard to the disposition made of the bridge bonds, 582; Mr. Bushnell received a part of the bonds, 583; after the act of Congress of Feuruary 24, 1871, a new bond was issued, bearing 8 per cent. interest, and the old issue was withdrawn, 583; the new bonds were sold to C. S. Bushnell, 583; the bonds were sold at about 80; the Union Pacific Company's books show that the company received $2,050,000 for them, 583; Bushnell arranged the loans in New York for the company, 583; 125 bonds were delivered to the trustees of the Omaha bridge bond, 583; they were afterwards sent to London, and there sold, 583; A. E. T. Sickles was general superintendent on the 21st of March, 1872, 584; the charges on the Omaha bridge is 50 cents for each passenger, and $10 a car for freight, 584; the same rates are charged for the transportation of Government freight, 584; there is a separate account kept at Omaha of the moneys received from the bridge, 584; the income bonds were issued pursuant to a resolution of the executive committee, adopted September 23, 1869, 584; copy of the resolution, 584; disposition made of the income bonds, 585; copy of the checks referred to in the testimony of Mr. Spence, 585; I indorsed all the checks as secretary, 586; amount paid Rollins and charged to legal expense account, 586; the services I rendered were in adjustment of accounts of the company and the Departments at Washington, and also with reference to matters pending before Congress, 587; the company is receiving coal from the Wyoming Coal Company, since 1869, 587; the company pays 7 per cent. per annum and commission, 588; amount due John Duff and Oliver Ames, 589; executive committee resolution in relation to stocks, bonds, and securities, 589; amount of collaterals placed in the hands of Mr. Clark, 589; all the securities of the company are held as collateral, 589; copy of telegram sent by Sickles to Rolling, 590; corrected statement of the bonds of the company, 590; copy of the agreement between Union Pacific Railroad Company and George W. Homans, jr., of Omaha, 590; copy of contract Union Pacific Railroad Company with C. O. Godfrey and Thomas Wardell, 591; detailed statement of bills payable, January 31, 1873, 593; notes due in April, 1873, 594; notes due in May, 1873, 594; memorandum showing the liability of the company to the persons named, 595; list of directors from 1869 to 1872, 596, 597, 598; copy of list of stockholders used at the annual election, 1863, 599, 600, 601; [illegible]

OLLINS, E. H.—Continued.

604; list of subscribers to the capital stock of the Union Pacific Railroad, 604; stockholders Union Pacific Railroad, and number of shares standing in their respective names at the closing of transfer-books, February 24, 1872, 601, 602, 603, list of stockholders of the Union Pacific Railroad at the close of business, February 26, 1870, 605; list of subscribers to the capital stock Union Pacific Railroad, 607; list of stockholders Union Pacific Railroad February 25, 1871, 607; list of subscribers to the capital stock Union Pacific Railroad, shares $1,000 each, 611; disposition made of income-bonds, 611; statement of income-bonds exchanged for certificates for first-mortgage bonds, 611; detailed statement of the persons who received the 8,263 land-grant bonds sold under resolution of April 9, 1869, 613; United States 6 per cent. 30-year bonds; abstract from ledger, 615; abstract Ledger C, 616; abstract from Ledger A, 617; United States 6 per cent. 30-year currency bonds on hand; abstract Ledger B, 618; first-mortgage bonds, abstract Ledger A, 619, 620, 621; first-mortgage bonds; abstract Ledger B, 622, 623; first-mortgage bonds, abstract Ledger C, 624; land-grant bonds, 626; income-bonds, 627; action taken by the board in relation to the disposition of the land-grant bonds, 638; amount realized by the company from each class of bonds issued and received, 639.

RICE, JOHN A., testimony of:

Stock issued in the name of Rice, 294; stock issued to B. E. Bates as treasurer of the trustees under the Ames and Davis contracts, 294; paid the money to the treasurer for the shares, 294; assistant treasurer of the trustees, 294; did not leave any money with the treasurer, 294; name signed for 120,000 shares of stock, amounting to $12,000,000, 294.

S.

SCOTT, THOMAS A., testimony of:

Was president of the Union Pacific Railroad from March, 1871, until March, 1872, 649; I was at the meeting on the 9th of March; the committee heard Mr. Bushnell's claims, as stated by myself, and granted him the amount of $126,000, 650; Bushnell gave me a check for $19,000; this check I deposited on my return to Philadelphia, at the Girard bank, 651.

SHAW, W. BIGLER, testimony of:

Newspaper correspondent, 220; was aware of the steps taken by the Secretary of the Treasury, 220; ascertained the fact from the Secretary himself, 220; conversation between Boutwell and Shaw, 221; before the stock fell I unloaded, 221; I gave two hundred dollars to R. J. Hinton, 223; am always more or less dabbling in stocks, 223; brokers carried stock for me, 224; I do not think it is a part of the business of this committee to inquire into my private transactions, 224. I think Mr. Clews carried stock for me, 225.

SHERMAN, CHARLES T., testimony of:

I was one of the Government directors, 651; the route mentioned in the Williams report was the one adopted, 651; the Black Hills route was fully known to the directors at the time of letting the Ames contract, 651; we condemned the Hoxie contract at the first meeting of the board in New York, 652; but afterward, when we discovered that the executive committee had extended the Hoxie contract 150 miles farther, without submitting it to the board, and without communicating or reporting it to the board for nearly a year afterward, we did feel disposed to protest and take some action on the subject, but why we did not I cannot give the reasons now; we felt outraged at the time, 652; the ground of objection was that the price was too large, too extravagant; it was $50,000 a mile, but it should not have cost the half of that, 52; the price stated at which the Oakes Ames contract was let per mile, 653; I think the prices paid Ames were double what they should have been, 654; the Hoxie contract was extended while I was a director, 655; we knew that the Hoxie contract had been assigned to the Credit Mobilier, of which a large number of the directors were members, 655; by a report of June, 1865, we set out the Hoxie contract in full to the Secretary of the Interior, and stated our objections to it; after which we acquiesced in it, 656; I had a general knowledge that the capital stock was not subscribed, only just the minimum amount, 656; the Boomer contract I never saw, and I do not recollect the particulars of the Hoxie contract, 657; in 1864 our compensation was fixed at so much per day, 657; I cannot say that I have experience in railroad-building, 658; I think the profit was a good deal more than fifteen millions, 659; I should treat the Government

ROLLINS, E. H.—Continued.

$14,550,278.94, 182; payment of $2,000.000, 182; consideration for which the $2,000,000 note was given, 182; additional charges on the Hoxie contract, 183; testimony relating to the $2,000,000 note, 183; an order to issue $16,000,000 additional bonds, 183; copy of preamble and resolutions, 184, 185; the $2,000,000 note and additional bond issue, 185; collateral security for the redemption of the bonds, 185; amount of bonds lost, 185; cost of the construction of the road covered by the Ames contract, 186; item charged to the Ames contract, 186; entry copied from the journal, 186; cost of the Davis contract, 187; copied from the books showing the cost of construction under the various contracts—Ames contract. Davis contract, and Hoxie contract, 187, 188; total cost of road to the Union Pacific Railroad Company, 188; amount of first-mortgage bonds issued by the Union Pacific Railroad Company, 188; land-grant bonds issued, 188: the Union Pacific Railroad Company does not owe the Credit Mobilier, 188; the Credit Mobilier indebted to the Union Pacific Railroad, 188, 189: present board of directors Union Pacific Railroad, 189; the company owes money to its directors, 189; special legal expenses, 189; resolution appointing a committee to audit legal expenses, 189, 190; testimony relating to legal expenses, including item of $126,000, 190, 191, 192, 193; the Union Pacific Railroad Company contract with the Pullman Car Company, 193, 194; the Harlan $10,000 legal-expense item of $126,000, and money to influence elections, 195; property belonging to the Union Pacific Railroad in the possession of the treasurer, 196; statement of assets, 197; loans in which the Union Pacific Railroad has an interest, 198, 199; net earnings for the last year $4,000,000, 199; the Government 5 per cent. comes in when the road is completed, 200; claim against the Government for transportation, 200; gross and net earnings, 200, 201; statement of the indebtedness of the Union Pacific Railroad, 210; statement of notes payable December 10, 1872, 210; notes due in January, 211; notes due in February, 211: notes due in March, 212; notes due in April, 212; demand notes, 212; statement of all the current indebtedness of the company, 212; Omaha bridge bonds, 224; the earnings on the bridge are ample to pay the interest on the bonds, 213; in favor of the Government recognizing the road as completed, 213; amount required to complete the road, 214; land-grant bonds, 214: the average price per acre for which lands were sold, $1.25 6/100, 214: the road will need for the present the same assistance it had in the past, 214, 215; estimated time that rails will last, from seven to ten years, 215: permanent counsel in the employ of the road, and salaries paid, 216; examined with reference to the $126,000, 216, 217: special attorneys employed, 218; corrected statement of Mr. Rollins, 219; the indenture under which the Omaha bridge bonds were issued bears date 1st day of November, A. D. 1870, 582; resolution in regard to the disposition made of the bridge bonds, 582; Mr. Bushuell received a part of the bonds, 583; after the act of Congress of Feuruary 24, 1871, a new bond was issued, bearing 8 per cent. interest, and the old issue was withdrawn, 583: the new bonds were sold to C. S. Bushnell, 583; the bonds were sold at about 80: the Union Pacific Company's books show that the company received $2,050,000 for them, 583; Bushnell arranged the loans in New York for the company, 583; 1,275 bonds were delivered to the trustees of the Omaha bridge bond, 583; they were afterwards sent to London, and there sold, 583; A. E. T. Sickles was general superintendent on the 21st of March, 1872, 584; the charges on the Omaha bridge is 50 cents for each passenger, and $10 a car for freight, 584; the same rates are charged for the transportation of Government freight, 584; there is a separate account kept at Omaha of the moneys received from the bridge, 584; the income bonds were issued pursuant to a resolution of the executive committee, adopted September 23, 1869, 584; copy of the resolution, 584; disposition made of the income-bonds, 585; copy of the checks referred to in the testimony of Mr. Spence, 585; I indorsed all the checks as secretary, 586; amount paid Rollins and charged to legal expense account, 586; the services I rendered were in adjustment of accounts of the company and the Departments at Washington, and also with reference to matters pending before Congress, 587; the company is receiving coal from the Wyoming Coal Company, since 1869, 587; the company pays 7 per cent. per annum and commission, 588; amount due John Duff and Oliver Ames, 589; executive committee resolution in relation to stocks, bonds, and securities, 589; amount of collaterals placed in the hands of Mr. Clark, 589; all the securities of the company are held as collateral, 589; copy of telegram sent by Sickles to Rolling, 590; corrected statement of the bonds of the company, 590; copy of the agreement between Union Pacific Railroad Company and George W. Homans, jr., of Omaha, 590; copy of contract Union Pacific Railroad Company with C. O. Godfrey and Thomas Wardell, 591; detailed statement of bills payable, January 31, 1873, 593; notes due in April, 1873, 594; notes due in May, 1873, 594; momorandum showing the liability of the company to the persons named, 595; list of directors from 1869 to 1872, 596, 597, 598, 599. copy of list of stockholders used at the annual election, 1863, 599, 600, 601; list

CPSIA information can be obtained
at www.ICGtesting.com
Printed in the USA
LVHW021147290323
742728LV00002B/222

9 781358 227646